Practical First Aid

DORLING KINDERSLEY
London • New York • Sydney • Moscow
www.dk.com

Principles of first aid

What is first aid?

This is the first assistance or treatment that is given to a casualty. First aid may be administered by a bystander, a relative or by a professional medical person and is often the most important help that a casualty receives. Once first aid has been given, the first aider may need to arrange for secondary aid such as a doctor or an ambulance.

The aims of first aid are:

- To preserve life.
- To prevent the casualty's injury becoming worse.
- To promote recovery.

The first aider's tasks are:

- To find out what has happened.
- To be aware of any dangers and deal with them appropriately.
- To deal calmly and efficiently with an injury or condition.
- To arrange the next stage of the casualty's care; this may mean making sure that the casualty can get home, advising rest or arranging for the casualty to get to hospital.

What equipment is necessary?

First aid requires no special equipment, although a first aid kit is useful (see p. 30). A good first aider is resourceful and will be able to utilise the items that are available.

British Red Cross note

Because of the practical nature of this book, some of the first aid procedures shown are simplified versions of the current practice at the time of publication. The book is a useful tool for all first aiders, however, a book cannot be a substitute for actual training. For further information on training courses contact your local office of the British Red Cross.

A DORLING KINDERSLEY BOOK
www.dk.com

Project Editor Claire Cross
Art Editor Glenda Fisher
Designer Lucy Parissi

Senior Editor Penny Warren
Senior Art Editor Karen Ward

Managing Editor Jemima Dunne
Managing Art Editor Lynne Brown

Production Louise Daly

Photography Andy Crawford

British Red Cross consultants Anita Kerwin-Nye and Lyn Covey

First published in Great Britain in 1998

Revised edition published in 1999 by Dorling Kindersley Limited, 9 Henrietta Street, Covent Garden, London WC2E 8PS

2 4 6 8 10 9 7 5 3

A CIP catalogue record for this book is available from the British Library

ISBN 0-7513-1963-5

Reproduced by Colourscan, Singapore
Printed by Wing King Tong, Hong Kong

Contents

Coping with accidents 4

Breathing and circulation 12

First aid materials 30

Disorders of consciousness 38

Wounds and bleeding 48

Burns and scalds 60

Bone, joint and muscle injuries 68

Poisoning 80

Effects of temperature 86

Small foreign bodies 90

Coping with Accidents

When faced with an accident, you should first assess whether the scene of the accident is safe, then assess any injuries; only after that decide what action to take. Whatever the situation, it is important that you are calm and confident, particularly when you are with the casualties, as this will reassure them.

DEALING WITH CASUALTIES

When you are sure that the area is safe, try to locate all the casualties; some may have been thrown some distance or have wandered away. If there is more than one casualty, decide who is the most seriously injured (see p. 11) and treat him first. Try to keep bystanders back until the emergency services say it is safe to go near.

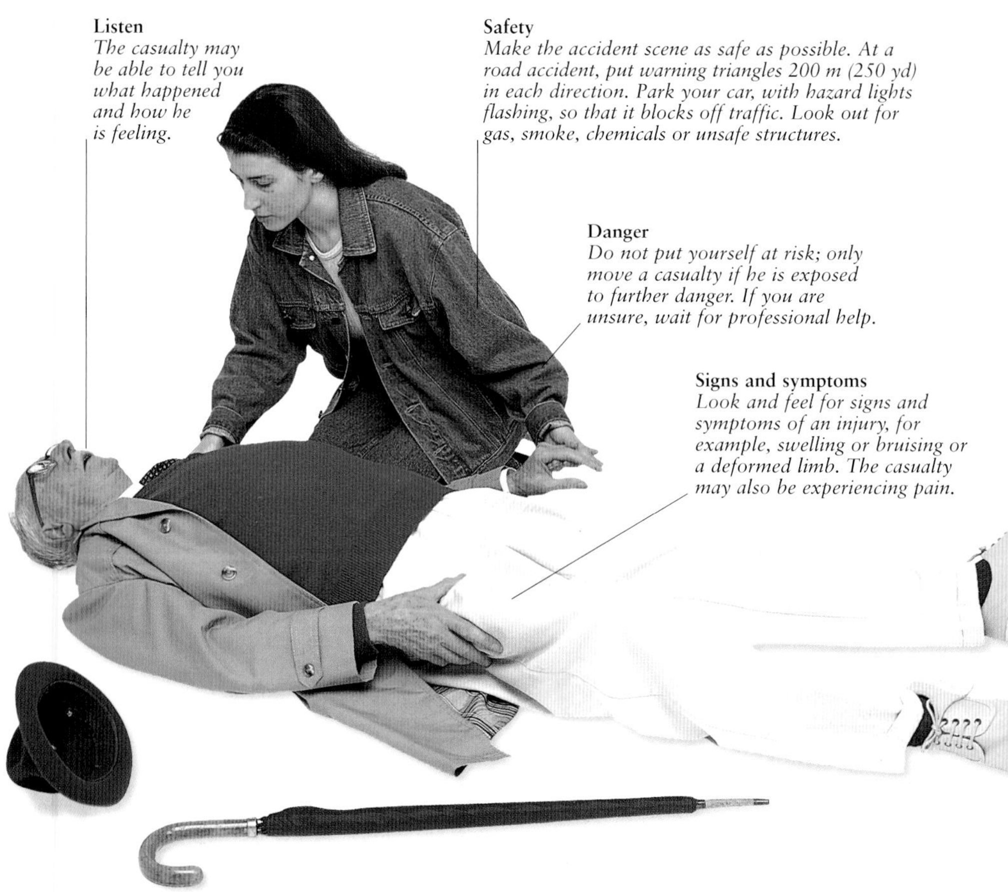

Listen
The casualty may be able to tell you what happened and how he is feeling.

Safety
Make the accident scene as safe as possible. At a road accident, put warning triangles 200 m (250 yd) in each direction. Park your car, with hazard lights flashing, so that it blocks off traffic. Look out for gas, smoke, chemicals or unsafe structures.

Danger
Do not put yourself at risk; only move a casualty if he is exposed to further danger. If you are unsure, wait for professional help.

Signs and symptoms
Look and feel for signs and symptoms of an injury, for example, swelling or bruising or a deformed limb. The casualty may also be experiencing pain.

IMPORTANT
Make sure that you are not putting yourself at risk by approaching an incident or casualty.

MOTOR VEHICLES

- Check the surrounding area: a casualty may have been thrown clear of a car or have walked away in a state of shock.
- Look out for hazard warning signs on a vehicle. If you don't know what a sign means keep your distance, particularly if there is a spillage on the road.
- Do not try to move a casualty who is trapped in a vehicle unless he is in immediate danger. Turn off the ignition and call an ambulance immediately.
- Do not smoke or allow any bystanders to smoke near a crashed vehicle.

MOTORBIKES OR BICYCLES

- Do not move the casualty unless he is in immediate danger.
- Do not remove helmets; leave it to the emergency services. However, if you need to give artificial ventilation (see p. 20), undo or cut the straps and, with a helper keeping the head and neck supported and aligned with the spine, gently ease the helmet over the top of the head.
- Keep the casualty warm and as comfortable as possible.

MAKING A DIAGNOSIS

- Check casualties who are very quiet first; these are often the most seriously injured and require the most urgent attention.
- History – ask the bystanders or the casualty, if he is conscious, how the accident happened.
- Signs and symptoms – if a casualty is conscious ask him to try to describe any symptoms. Look for signs of injury such as bleeding or burns (see panel, opposite).

You need to:

Look out for danger

Check for any hazards before you approach a casualty. If in danger, do not approach a casualty.

Follow the ABC of resuscitation

If the casualty appears unconscious check his responses (see p. 16); if unconscious, open the airway and check breathing; if breathing, put in the recovery position. Check the circulation. Keep the airway open. Be ready to resuscitate (see pp. 16–25).

Get help, if necessary

If necessary, call the emergency services. Ideally, get someone else to call while you stay with the casualty.

Treat the most serious conditions first

Deal with conditions that could cause shock to develop, such as major bleeding (see p. 48) or serious burns (see p. 63). Watch for signs of shock and treat accordingly (see p. 51).

Support broken bones

If possible, stabilise and support suspected broken bones (see p. 71).

Treat any minor injuries found

Deal with any other injuries. Constantly reassure the casualty.

MAJOR HAZARDS

It is vital that you do not become a casualty yourself while you are helping an injured person. Some incidents are especially dangerous, for example, the casualty may still be in contact with a source of electricity, or he may be near a fire or in an accident involving a vehicle carrying dangerous chemicals. In these situations, follow the advice given below.

ELECTRICAL INJURIES

If the casualty is in contact with electricity, stop the current at once by switching it off at the mains or pulling out the plug. If this is not possible, get the casualty's limb away from the electrical contact: stand on a dry surface, such as wood, a folded newspaper or a rubber mat, and carefully knock the limb clear with a similar material.

- ▶ **DO NOT** attempt first aid until the contact has been broken.
- ▶ **DO NOT** touch anything wet because water conducts electricity.

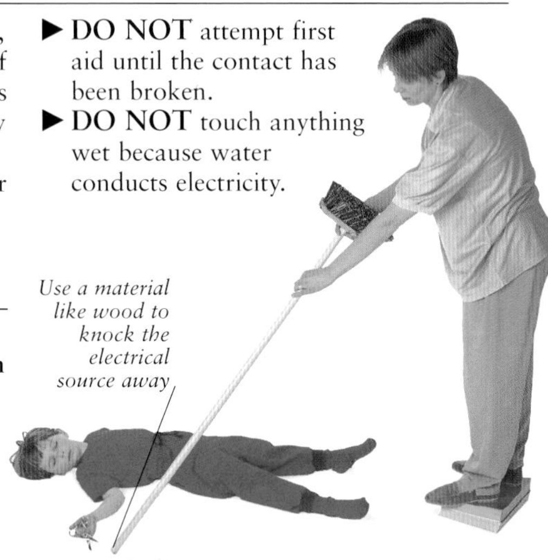

Use a material like wood to knock the electrical source away

IMPORTANT

High-voltage electricity, for example, from overhead cables is extremely powerful. If a casualty is touching, or near, these cables, do not approach him before you have been officially told that it has been switched off and that the area is safe. Stay at least 18 m (20 yd) away; call the police.

FIRE

If you are confronted by a fire at home or in the street, act quickly and precisely. Call the emergency services, giving as much information as possible. If trapped in a room, shut the door, open a window and try to get out through the window as quickly as possible; lower yourself by your arms and drop feet first. If a person is on fire, follow the *Stop*, *Drop*, *Wrap*, *Roll* procedure described on page 62.

- ▶ **DO NOT** enter a smoke-filled room or building: there is a serious danger of your being overcome by smoke or being badly burnt. If you have to pass through a burning room, keep close to the ground where the air is clearest.
- ▶ **DO NOT** attempt to put a big fire out. If in any doubt about your safety, call the emergency services, wait for them to arrive and do not put yourself at risk.

CHEMICAL SPILLS

Accidents may be complicated by the spillage of dangerous substances. Vans and lorries carrying chemicals display panels that indicate what they are carrying, its properties, a special code number and a telephone number. Pass these details on to the emergency services.

- ▶ **DO NOT** attempt a rescue unless you are sure that you will not come into contact with the hazardous substance.
- ▶ **DO NOT** approach a vehicle that is carrying toxic chemicals; if visible, note the details on the panel and give them to the emergency services.

TRANSPORTING THE INJURED

When you move a casualty, his or her safety and well-being should be your first consideration. Never move a casualty who you think may be seriously injured unless there is an immediate threat to the casualty's life; wait for professional help to arrive. If you have to move a casualty, support the joints above and below any suspected break (see p. 68) or other serious injury before you begin.

PRINCIPLES OF LIFTING

If you observe the following guidelines carefully, you will find yourself able to lift fairly heavy objects without undue strain. Remember, however, never try to move a person by yourself if there are people available to help and do not practise lifting anything or anyone heavier than yourself.

- Stand with your feet slightly apart to maintain a stable, balanced posture.
- Straighten your back and bend the knees.
- Use your thigh, hip and shoulder muscles to take as much of the weight as possible.
- Keep the weight of the casualty's body as close to your body as possible.

DRAGGING A CASUALTY TO SAFETY

If danger makes it necessary to move a person, the drag method is a quick way to transport an unconscious casualty to safety or to move a conscious casualty who is unable to walk, however, avoid this method if you suspect an injury to the head or neck.

Approach the casualty from behind and fold one of her arms across her chest (use an uninjured arm). Slide your arms beneath her armpits and then grasp both her arms. If possible, get a bystander to steady the casualty's head and keep it in line with her body while you drag her.

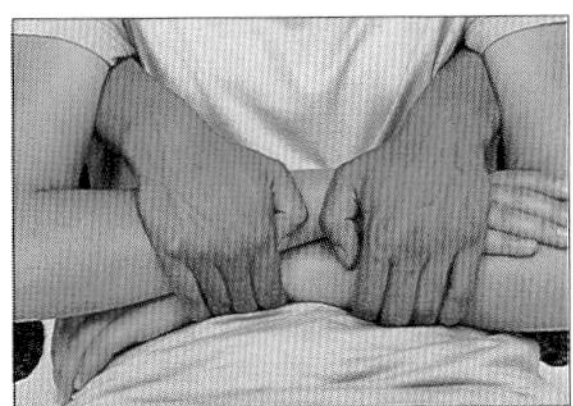

Place your hands over the casualty's arms.

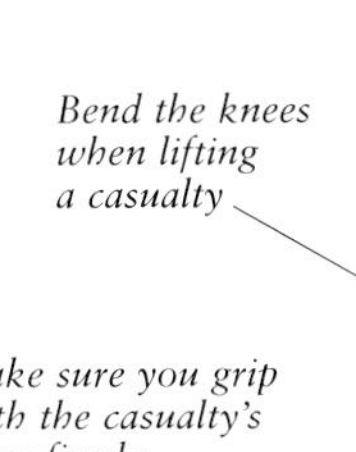

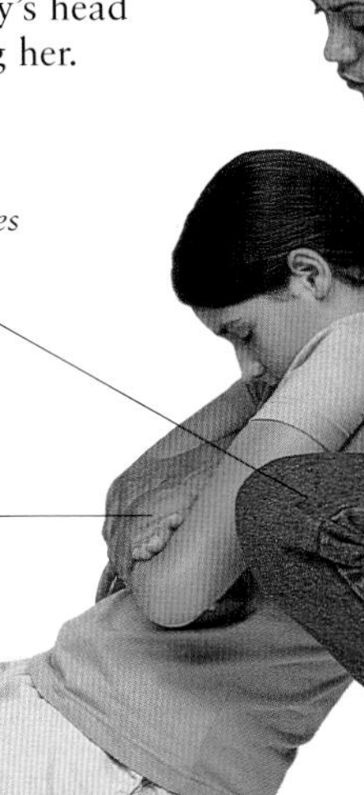

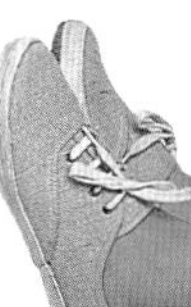

Bend the knees when lifting a casualty

Make sure you grip both the casualty's arms firmly

Dealing with body fluids

Certain viruses, such as human immunodeficiency virus (HIV) and Hepatitis B, are transmitted via blood to blood contact, for example, if an infected person's blood comes into contact with an open sore. When treating a casualty, always handle body fluids as hygienically as possible to keep the risk of cross-infection to a minimum.

How to avoid cross-infection

There are several measures you can take to avoid cross-infection when dealing with body fluids. Follow the guidelines below to help to minimise the risk of infection when treating a casualty who is bleeding or when disposing of used dressings.

WASH HANDS

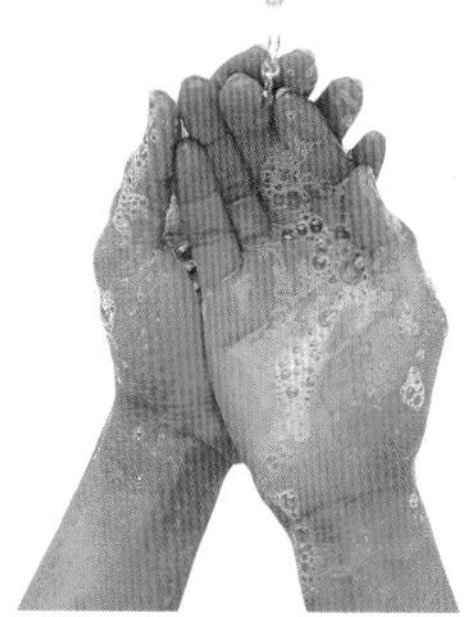

Whenever possible, wash your hands thoroughly before and after treating a casualty. Make sure you wash both the back and front of your hands.

WEAR GLOVES

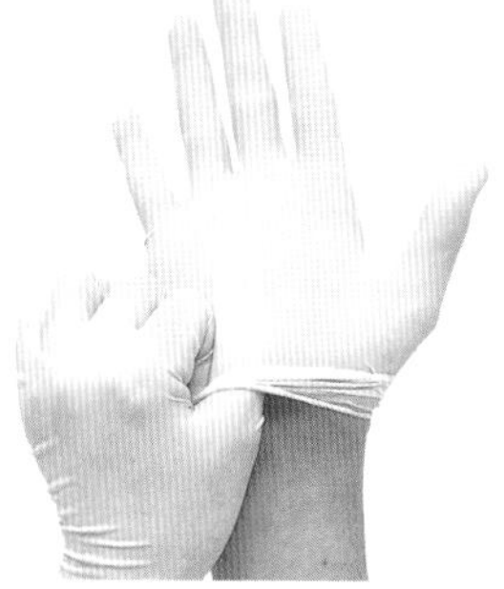

If available, wear disposable gloves whenever dealing with blood or applying or disposing of sterile dressings. Alternatively, cover your hands with clean plastic bags.

COVER WOUND

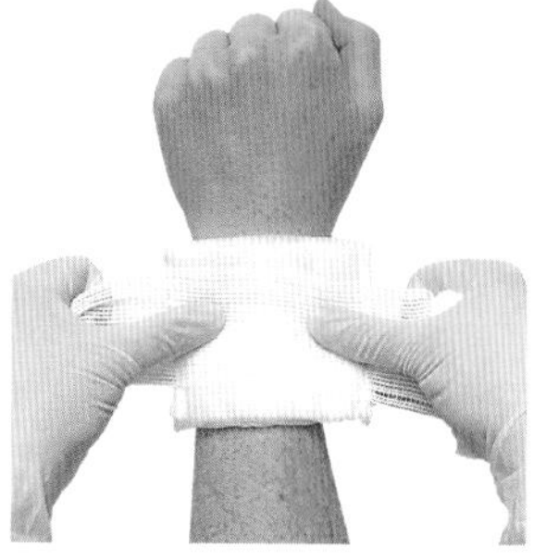

Cover a wound with a dressing making sure that you do not touch the inside sterile pad of the dressing. If possible, wear disposable gloves to apply dressings.

Disposing of waste

These yellow plastic containers are for used needles, hypodermic syringes and any other sharp objects. The yellow containers are then collected by authorised waste collectors to be disposed of safely.

Sharps container

After treating a casualty, get rid of used sterile dressings and waste products as soon as possible by placing them in a special marked, yellow bag. The bag should then be sealed and incinerated.

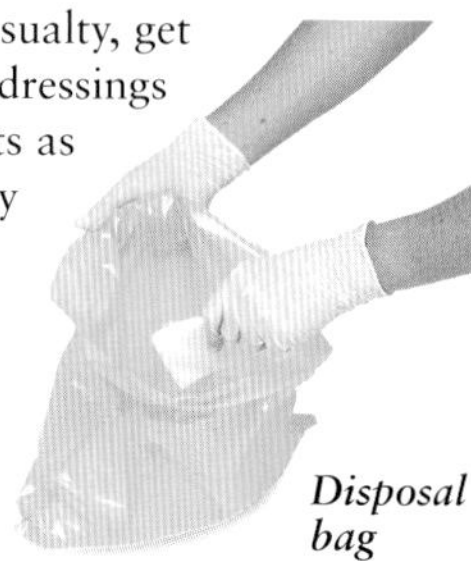

Disposal bag

GETTING HELP

Throughout this book, advice is given on the type of medical help to seek when you are treating a casualty. There are four categories as follows:

■ **ADVISE THE CASUALTY TO SPEAK TO A DOCTOR**
when follow-up treatment is advisable;

☎ **CALL A DOCTOR**
when advice on treatment is necessary;

☐ **TAKE OR SEND THE CASUALTY TO HOSPITAL**
when hospital treatment is necessary but you may be able to take the casualty;

✚ **CALL AN AMBULANCE**
when ambulance treatment is needed.

CALLING AN AMBULANCE

You can call an ambulance free from normal telephones and most mobile phones. Motorways have free phones at one-mile intervals that automatically connect you to the emergency services. To call an ambulance, follow these guidelines:

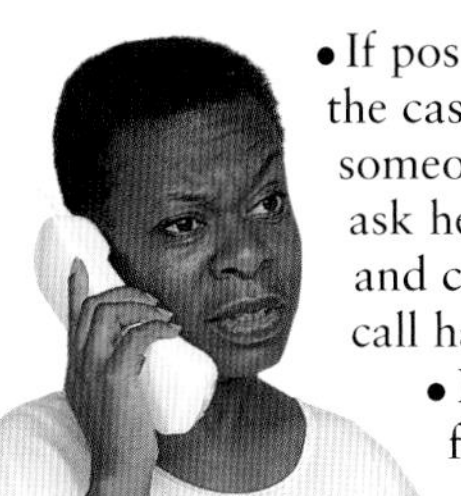

- If possible, stay with the casualty and send someone else to phone; ask her to come back and confirm that the call has been made.
- Dial 999 or 112 for the appropriate service; the officer can contact the other services.
- Give the telephone number of where the call is being made from.
- Give the location; landmarks; suspected cause; the number and approximate age of casualties and the extent of injuries.
- Replace the receiver after, and not before, the control officer does so.

STRESS

An emergency can be distressing, even for an experienced first aider. This is a natural reaction, particularly if you have been treating a badly injured casualty. The experience may also affect you later, so it is important to face up to how you feel about what has happened.

HOW YOU COPE

Many worry about how they will cope in an emergency, however, most do perfectly well. The body has a mechanism called "flight or fight" whereby, when faced with an emergency, hormones are released that prepare the body for a stressful situation. Too much stress, however, can affect how you cope; if you feel unable to cope, take slow, deep breaths to help you calm down. If this fails, ask someone else to take over.

HOW YOU FEEL

Depending on the incident and the outcome you may feel various emotions after treating a casualty, ranging from satisfaction with your actions to anger and confusion if the outcome is unclear or upsetting. Releasing these feelings straight after the event helps you to cope.

Talking to somone can help you to cope

EMERGENCY ACTION PLAN

When faced with an emergency you need to prioritise your actions to enable you to act as calmly and efficiently as possible. The chart below helps you to react sensibly in an emergency, to assess both the scene and any possible dangers and to deal with casualties efficiently.

ASSESS SCENE

1 DANGER
Are you in danger?

NO → Proceed to step 2

YES ↓

Can you eliminate the danger?

YES → Turn off a car ignition or electricity at the mains; kick broken glass out of the way.

NO ↓

Can you remove the casualty from danger without endangering yourself?

NO → If you are in any doubt about your own or a casualty's safety, **DO NOT** approach, CALL THE EMERGENCY SERVICES and then wait nearby until they arrive.

YES ↓

Move the casualty; you can use the "drag" method to safely move her. However, you should only move an injured casualty if she is in immedaite danger.

see *Dragging a casualty to safety* p. 7

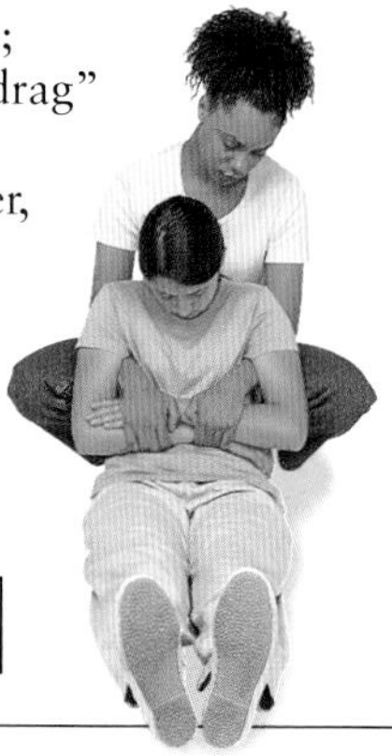

When to call for help

Call the emergency services as soon as possible with information on the type of incident, the number of casualties and their condition, for example, whether they are breathing, so that they can respond appropriately. If danger prevents you approaching a casualty, telephone for help; you can always ring back with more information. If possible, get a bystander to make the call while you stay with the casualty (see p. 9).

2 ASSESS CASUALTIES
Is there more than one casualty?

YES → When faced with a number of casualties, check the quietest ones first because they may be the most seriously injured.

NO ↓

Check response and follow the resuscitation sequence to treat airway or breathing difficulties (see pp. 16–25).

IF unconscious and NOT breathing →

- **✚ CALL AN AMBULANCE**
- If not breathing, give artificial ventilations; if no pulse, give CPR until help arrives (see pp. 20 and 22).

IF casualty resumes breathing ↓

IF conscious ↓

- Treat serious conditions such as major bleeding.
- Treat for shock if necessary (see p. 51).
- Treat minor injuries.

IF unconscious and breathing →

- Treat life-threatening conditions, such as major bleeding or burns.
- Put in recovery position.
- **✚ CALL AN AMBULANCE**
- Treat minor conditions.

Monitor the casualty's breathing and pulse and his responses to verbal and physical stimuli until help arrives; be ready to repeat the resuscitation procedure if necessary.

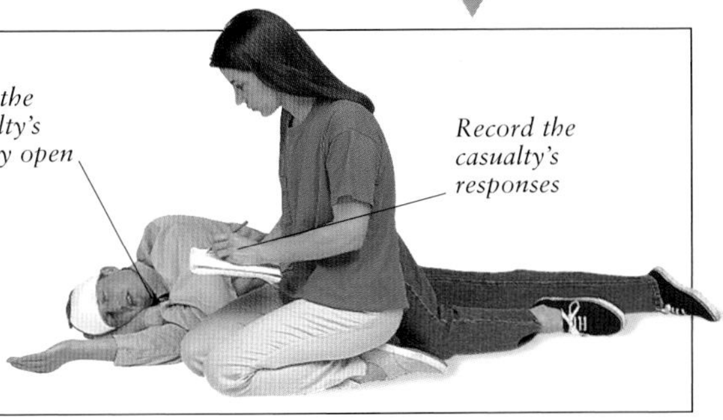

Keep the casualty's airway open

Record the casualty's responses

HAND OVER TO THE EMERGENCY SERVICES

As soon as the emergency services arrive, tell them how the casualty is and what treatment you have given.

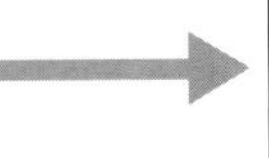

Seek help yourself if you feel that you need it.

BREATHING AND CIRCULATION

The body, and especially the brain, needs oxygen to sustain life and carry out bodily functions. Breathing is the process by which oxygen is taken from the air into the lungs (see p. 14); oxygen is then picked up by the blood and carried around the body via the circulatory system (see p. 15). If the body does not receive an adequate supply of oxygen, the casualty will lose consciousness and breathing and blood circulation will cease; urgent medical aid is then needed for oxygen to reach the brain.

DEALING WITH A COLLAPSED CASUALTY

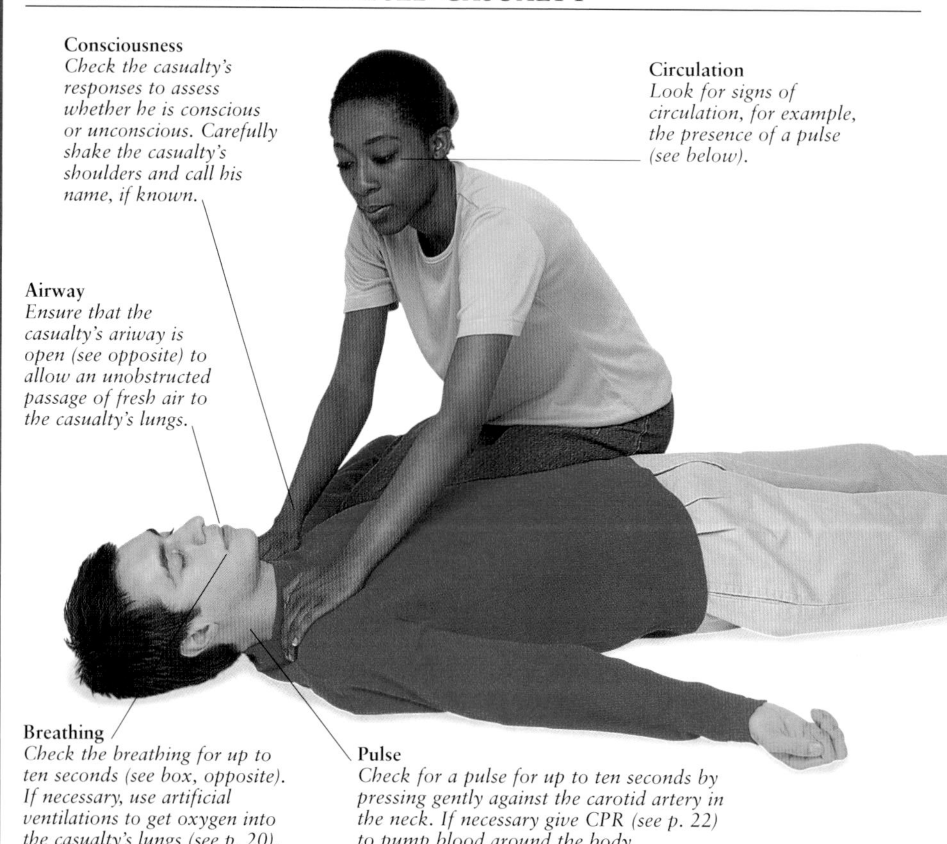

Consciousness
Check the casualty's responses to assess whether he is conscious or unconscious. Carefully shake the casualty's shoulders and call his name, if known.

Circulation
Look for signs of circulation, for example, the presence of a pulse (see below).

Airway
Ensure that the casualty's ariway is open (see opposite) to allow an unobstructed passage of fresh air to the casualty's lungs.

Breathing
Check the breathing for up to ten seconds (see box, opposite). If necessary, use artificial ventilations to get oxygen into the casualty's lungs (see p. 20).

Pulse
Check for a pulse for up to ten seconds by pressing gently against the carotid artery in the neck. If necessary give CPR (see p. 22) to pump blood around the body.

BREATHING PROBLEMS

When there is insufficient oxygen available to the body tissues, a condition called hypoxia can occur that can lead to unconsciousness and may be fatal. Hypoxia can be caused by:

- inadequate oxygen content in the air, for example, in a smoke-filled room;
- obstruction of the airway caused, for example, by choking (see p. 26);
- interference with, or paralysis of, the action of the muscles in the chest, for example, when a person's chest is buried in sand, or following electrocution.

ABC of resuscitation

When dealing with a collapsed casualty, follow the ABC of resuscitation shown below to assess whether the casualty is breathing and has a pulse.

A FOR AIRWAY

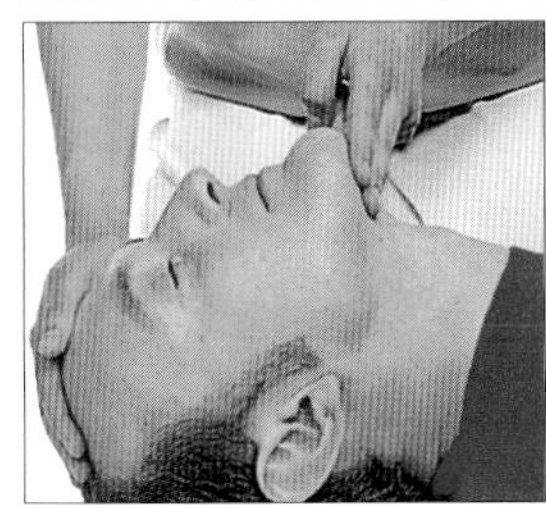

If the casualty is unconscious and lying on his back, the tongue may block the air passage (see below, left). Open the airway by lifting the chin with two fingers and pressing on the forehead to tilt the head back.

Airway blocked

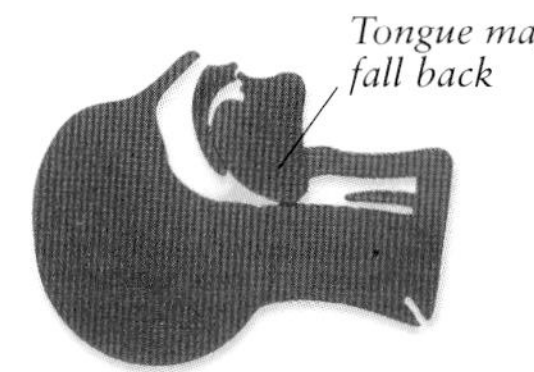

Airway open

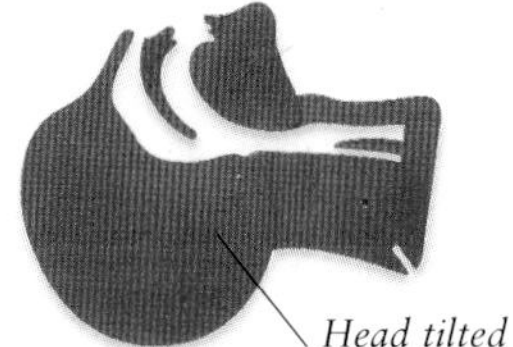

B FOR BREATHING

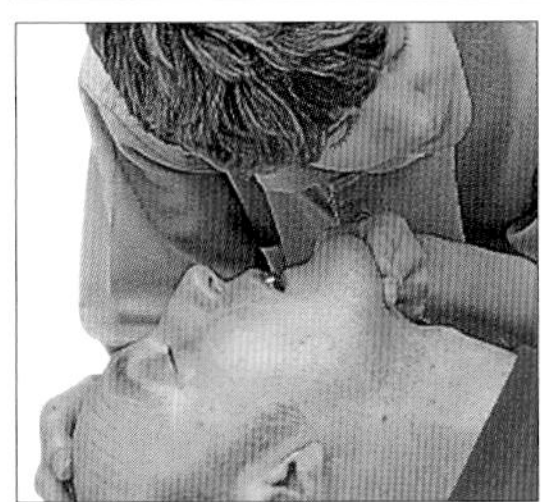

To find out whether or not a casualty is breathing, kneel down beside him and place your cheek as near his mouth as possible then look, listen and feel for any signs of breathing for up to ten seconds.

C FOR CIRCULATION

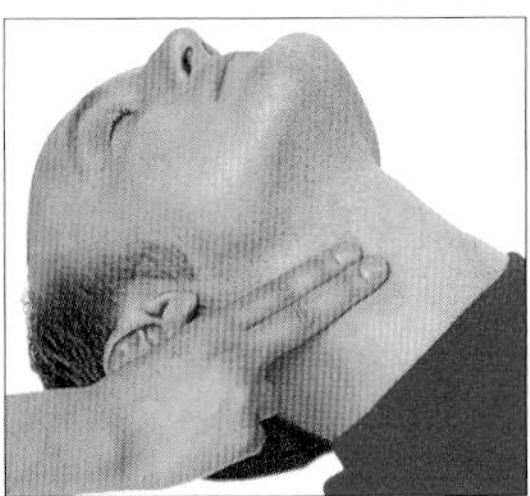

Check the casualty's circulation; feel for the carotid pulse in the neck (see p. 15) for an adult, or the brachial pulse in the arm for a baby (see p. 25). Look for other signs of circulation, such as a healthy skin colour.

RESPIRATORY SYSTEM

This consists of the nose, mouth, windpipe, lungs and the pulmonary blood vessels between the heart and lungs. It facilitates breathing and helps to provide energy by exchanging the gases, oxygen and carbon dioxide, in the lungs. Oxygen is breathed in and used by body cells to make energy and the waste product, carbon dioxide, is expelled in the air breathed out.

HOW WE BREATHE

When we breathe in, muscles in the chest and diaphragm contract, the chest enlarges and air with oxygen enters the body via the mouth and nose and passes into the windpipe (trachea), the tube that runs down the neck into the chest. The trachea divides into two smaller tubes (bronchi), one for each lung, which in turn subdivide into more tiny tubes (bronchioles) that end in microscopic air sacs; these form the bulk of the lungs and it is here that gases are exchanged (see above). To breathe out, muscles relax, the chest falls and the lungs are compressed sending used air up the windpipe and out of the body.

Cross-section of respiratory tract and lungs

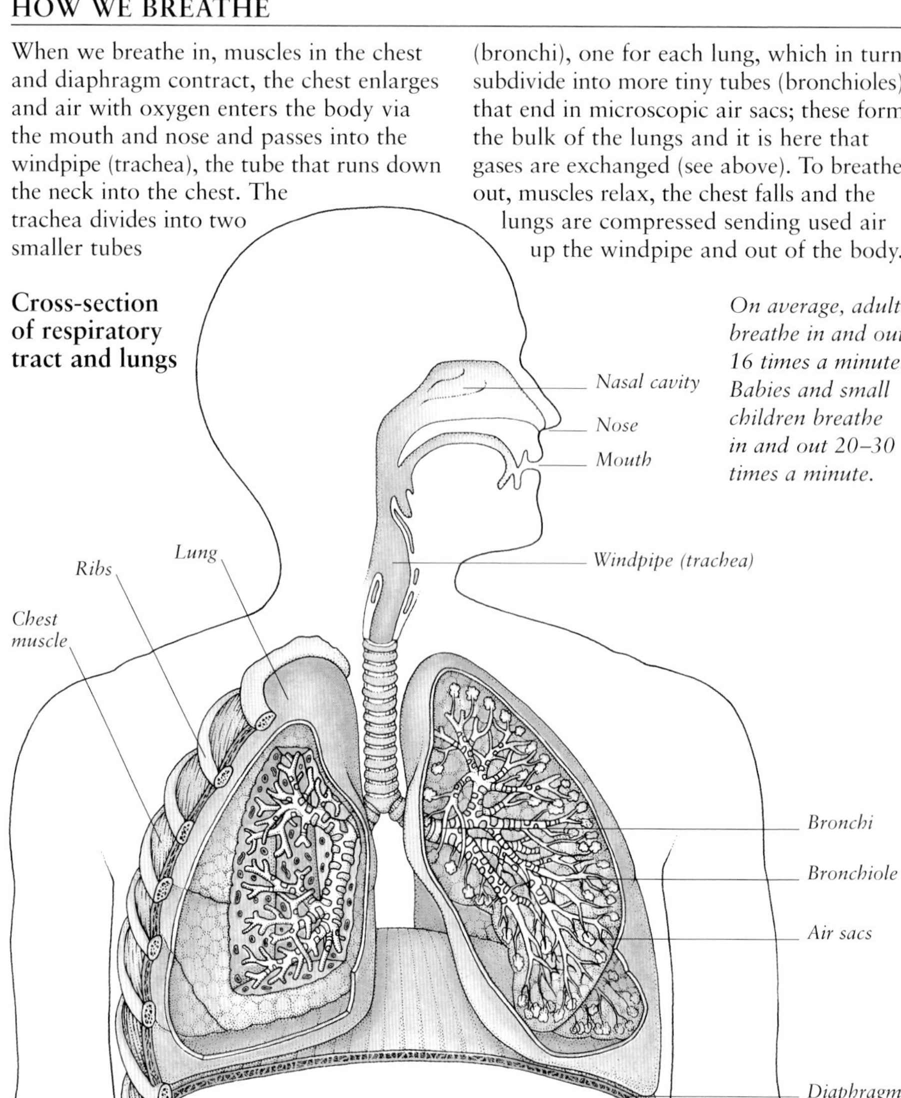

On average, adults breathe in and out 16 times a minute. Babies and small children breathe in and out 20–30 times a minute.

Circulatory system

The circulatory system comprises the heart and the blood vessels – veins, arteries and capillaries – that constantly circulate blood around the body. This continual flow of blood provides the body tissues with oxygen and nutrients and carries waste products, such as carbon dioxide, away from the body tissues to be expelled in the air breathed out.

HOW BLOOD CIRCULATES

The heart pumps blood into the main artery, the aorta; this divides into small arteries that travel around the body. Each small artery divides into tiny tubes called capillaries that in turn join up to form small veins to take blood back to the heart.

How gases are circulated

Bright red blood containing oxygen and nutrients is carried via arteries, then absorbed through the capillary walls to be used by the body tissues. Carbon dioxide is then picked up by the blood and veins take the blood, now dark red because it has little oxygen, back to the heart. The heart pumps the blood to the lungs where carbon dioxide is lost and oxygen taken up again (see opposite). Refreshed with oxygen and bright red again, blood returns to the heart and the cycle continues.

Diagram showing the passage of blood

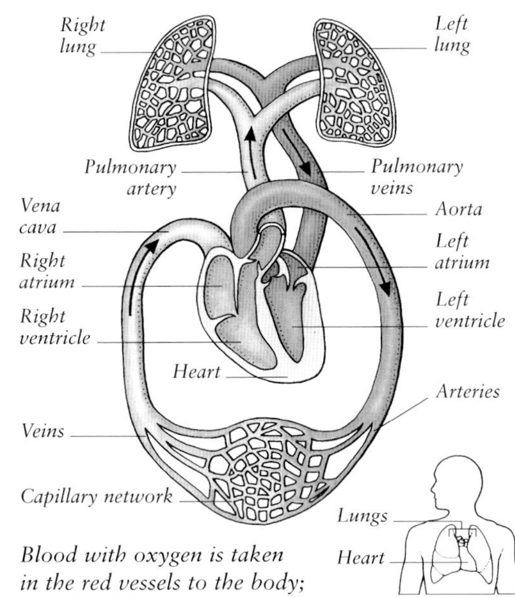

Blood with oxygen is taken in the red vessels to the body; blood with less oxygen returns to the lungs via the blue vessels.

Position of the heart and the lungs

The pulse

This throb or "beat" passes along an artery with each heartbeat. It is felt anywhere an artery is near skin, for example, at the wrist (radial) pulse. In an emergency, check the neck (carotid) pulse.

How to check the neck pulse

Press the middle and index finger in the hollow between the neck muscle and the Adam's apple; count the beats per minute and note whether the pulse is strong and regular. An adult heart beats 60–80 times a minute; a child's up to 100 times.

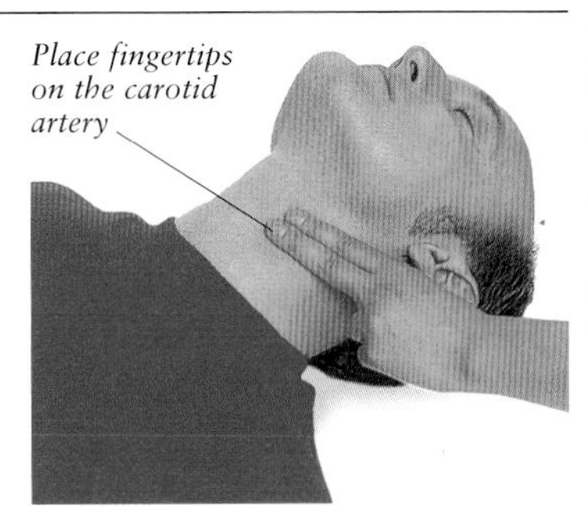

Place fingertips on the carotid artery

RESUSCITATION FOR AN ADULT

Follow the sequence below to ascertain if a collapsed casualty is conscious, breathing and has a heart beat (see ABC of resuscitation, p. 13) and to show you how to resuscitate him. For children and babies, see page 24.

1 Check the casualty's response

Check for danger then gently shake his shoulders. Talk to him to see if he responds. If no response, shout for help.

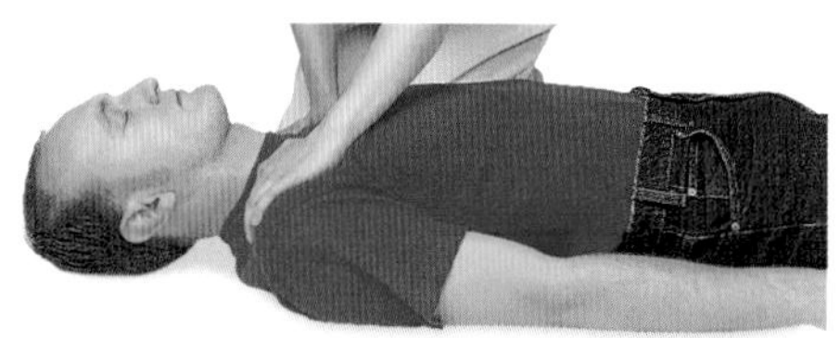

2 Open the airway and check breathing

Lift the chin and tilt the casualty's head back to keep the airway open. Check breathing for up to ten seconds (see p. 13).

IF the casualty is breathing, turn him into the recovery position (see p. 18).

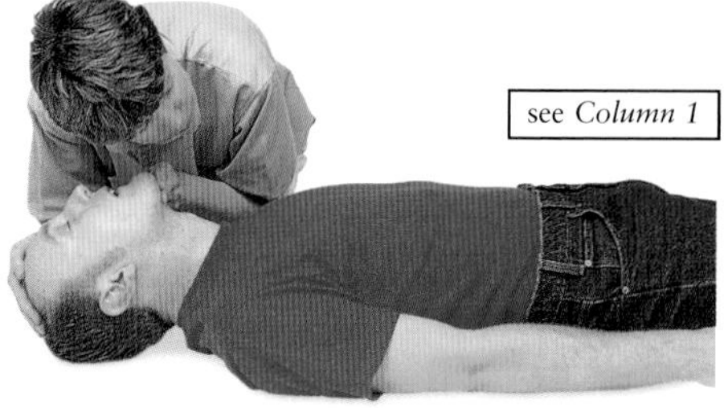

see *Column 1*

3 If there is no breathing, give artificial ventilation

Carefully remove any visible obstructions from the casualty's mouth, such as broken or loose dentures, however, do not try to remove well-fitting dentures. Keep the airway open by tilting the head back, then pinch the casualty's nostrils together and give two breaths (see p. 20).

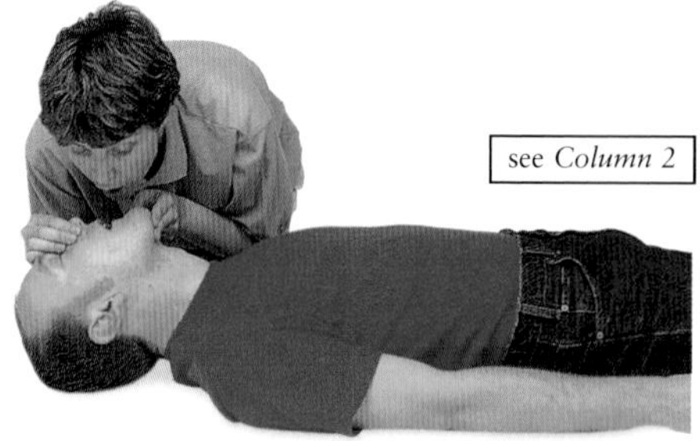

see *Column 2*

4 Check the circulation

Take the pulse for ten seconds to check the circulation (see p. 15). If a pulse is present, continue artificial ventilation.

IF there is no circulation, see step 5 below.

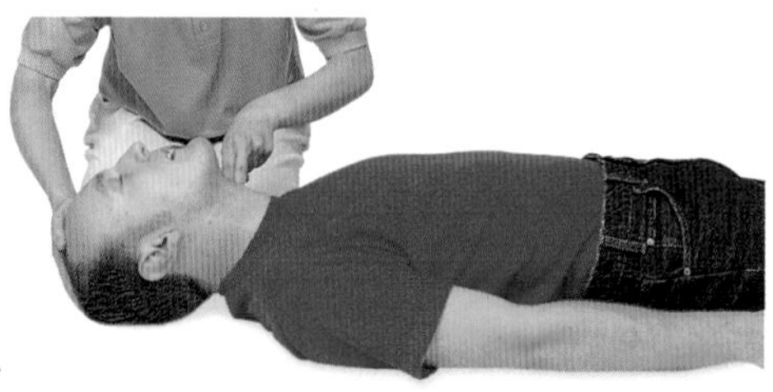

5 Give the casualty CPR

Combine chest compressions and artificial ventilations (see p. 22) until professional medical help arrives.

see *Column 3*

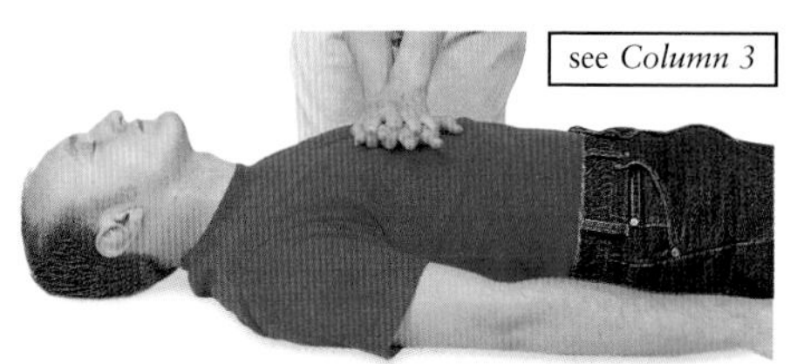

How you should respond

The resuscitation summary below is a quick reference guide to tell you how to respond to an unconscious casualty.

COLUMN 1

If unconscious, but breathing:

Deal with any life-threatening injuries such as severe bleeding.

Place the casualty in the recovery position (see p. 18).

✚ CALL AN AMBULANCE

IF possible, do not leave the casualty alone.

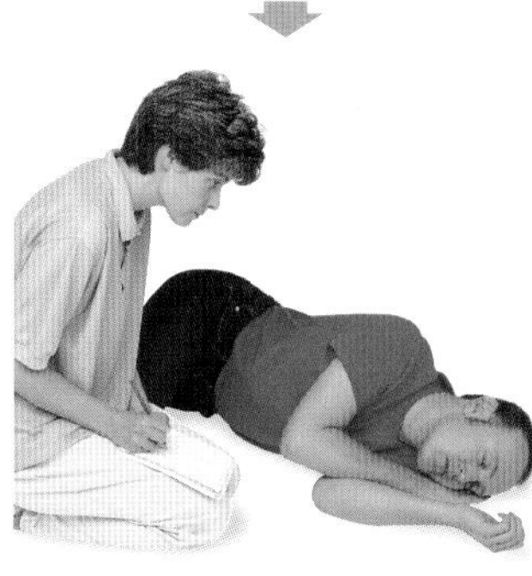

Monitor the casualty: regularly check breathing, circulation and response to speech and gentle physical stimulus.

COLUMN 2

If unconscious and not breathing:

✚ CALL AN AMBULANCE

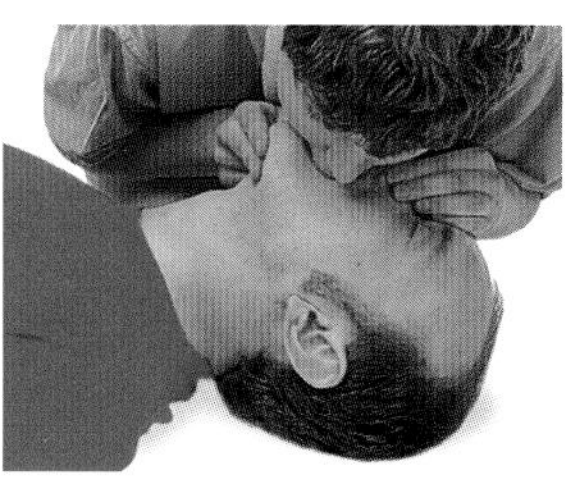

Give two breaths (see p. 20 for adults and p. 25 for children/babies).

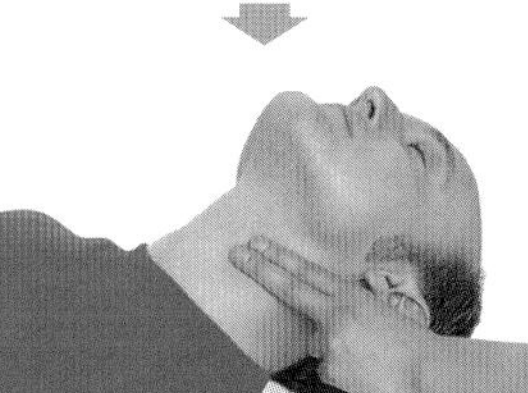

Check circulation (see p. 15).

IF the pulse is still present, give ventilations for one minute. Check the circulation after every minute.

Give ventilations until help arrives.

COLUMN 3

If there is no pulse or breathing:

✚ CALL AN AMBULANCE

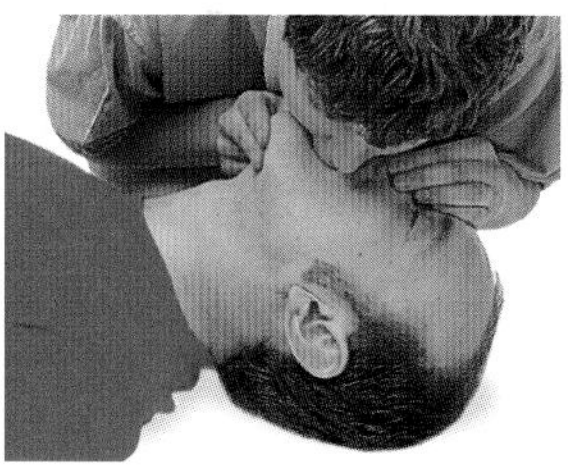

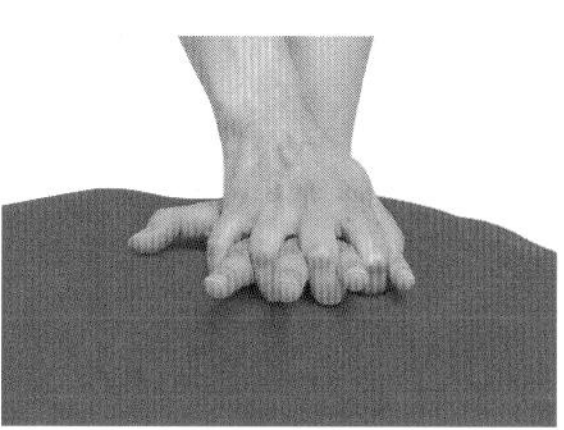

Give cardiopulmonary resuscitation (CPR). This is a combination of chest compressions and artificial ventilations (see p. 22 for adults and p. 25 for children/babies).

Continue giving the casualty CPR until the ambulance arrives. If someone trained to give CPR is with you, you should take it in turns to resuscitate the casualty.

THE RESUSCITATION SEQUENCE

A quick-reference guide

Open airway

Check for breathing for 10 seconds

IF casualty is breathing, place in recovery position (right)

IF casualty is not breathing

✚ CALL AN AMBULANCE

and continue sequence (below)

Give 2 breaths of artificial ventilation

Check the circulation

IF pulse present, give ventilations for 1 minute. Re-check the circulation every minute

IF pulse absent, give CPR at rate of 15 chest compressions to 2 ventilations

THE RECOVERY POSITION

An unconscious casualty who is breathing should be put in a recovery position. Put him in the position shown below or adapt this so that he is in a stable position on his side to prevent him choking on his tongue or vomit.

1 Keep the airway open

Kneel beside the casualty and open the airway by lifting the casualty's chin with two fingers and tilting his head back. Straighten the casualty's legs.

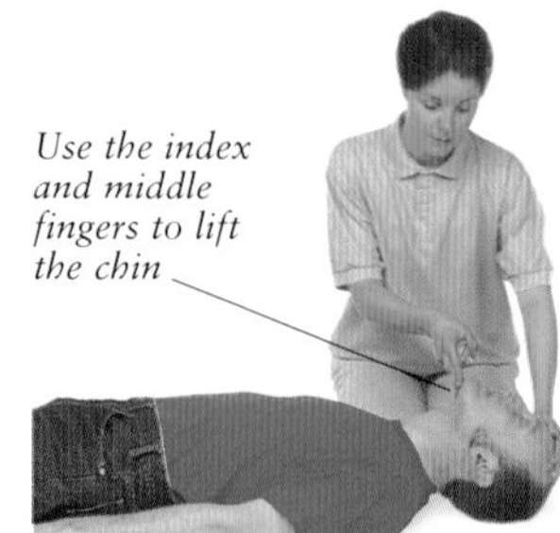

Use the index and middle fingers to lift the chin

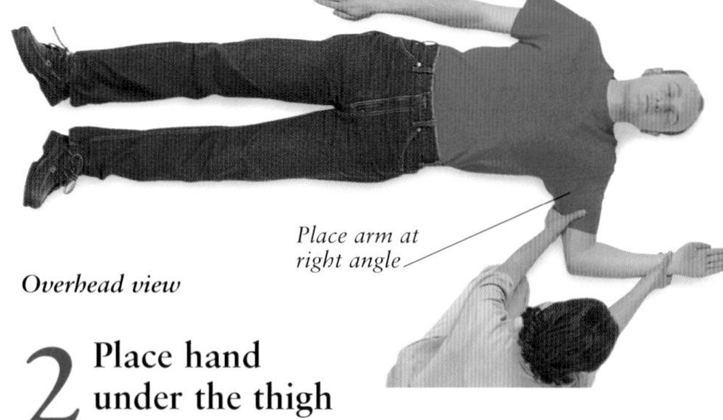

Place arm at right angle

Overhead view

2 Place hand under the thigh

Place the casualty's arm that is nearest to you at right angles to his body.

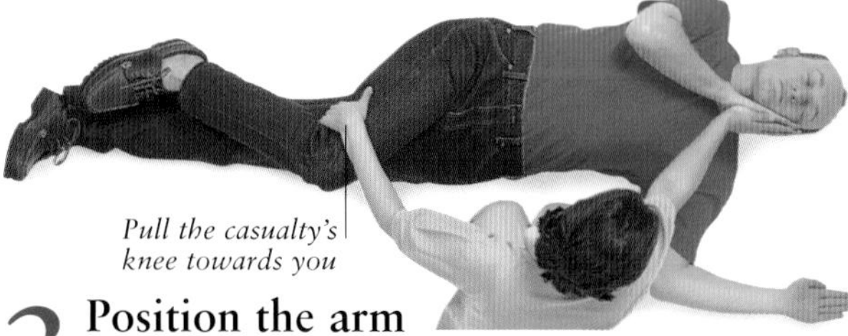

Pull the casualty's knee towards you

3 Position the arm and raise the leg

Bring the casualty's far arm across his chest and hold the hand, palm outwards, against his near cheek. With your other hand, grasp the thigh that is furthest from you and pull the knee up.

4 Pull the thigh towards you

With one hand, keep the casualty's hand pressed against his cheek to support his head and then pull his far thigh towards you, rolling the casualty on to his side.

Roll the leg right over

5 Place the leg at a right angle

Gently remove your hand from under the casualty's head and tilt his head back to keep the airway open. Pull the casualty's top leg up at right angles to the body to prevent it falling forwards.

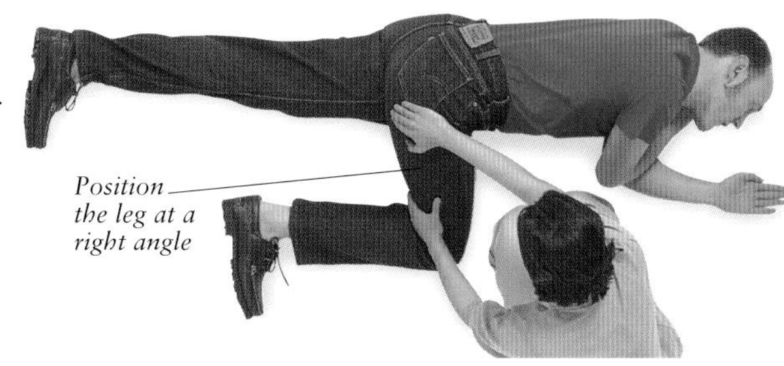

Position the leg at a right angle

6 Keep the airway open

Once the casualty is in the recovery position ensure that his airway remains open. If necessary, adjust the hand under his cheek.

✚ CALL AN AMBULANCE

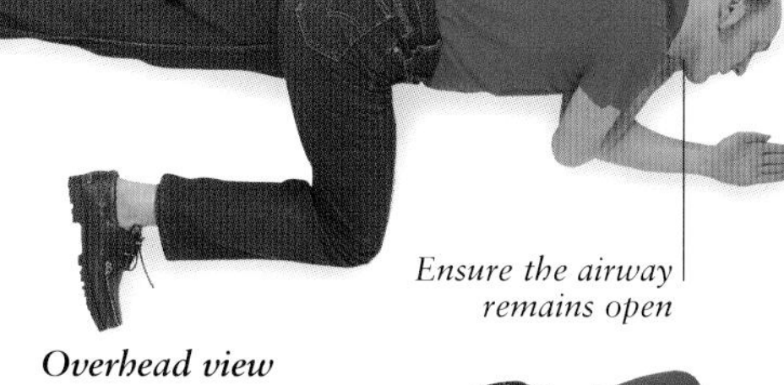

Ensure the airway remains open

Overhead view

Side view

7 Monitor the casualty

Check the casualty's breathing and circulation at regular frequent intervals while you wait for the ambulance.

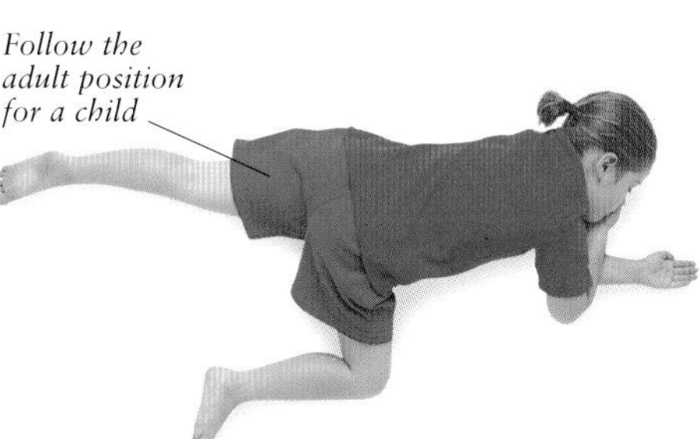

Follow the adult position for a child

IF an unconscious child over one year is breathing, open the airway and follow the adult recovery procedure above.

Cradle the baby in your arms

IF an unconscious baby under one year is breathing, open the airway and cradle him in your arms with his head downwards.

THE RESUSCITATION SEQUENCE

A quick-reference guide

Open airway

Check for breathing for 10 seconds

IF casualty is breathing, place in recovery position

IF casualty is not breathing

✚ CALL AN AMBULANCE

and continue sequence

Give 2 breaths of artificial ventilation (right)

Check the circulation (right)

IF pulse present, give ventilations for 1 minute. Re-check the circulation every minute (right)

IF pulse absent, give CPR at rate of 15 chest compressions to 2 ventilations

ARTIFICIAL VENTILATION

If the casualty is not breathing but has a pulse, give artificial ventilation (see below). If there is no breathing or pulse, give CPR (see p. 22).

1 Open the airway

Lift the chin and tilt the head back until you can see down the casualty's nostrils. Check the casualty's breathing for up to ten seconds.

IF there is no breathing,

✚ CALL AN AMBULANCE

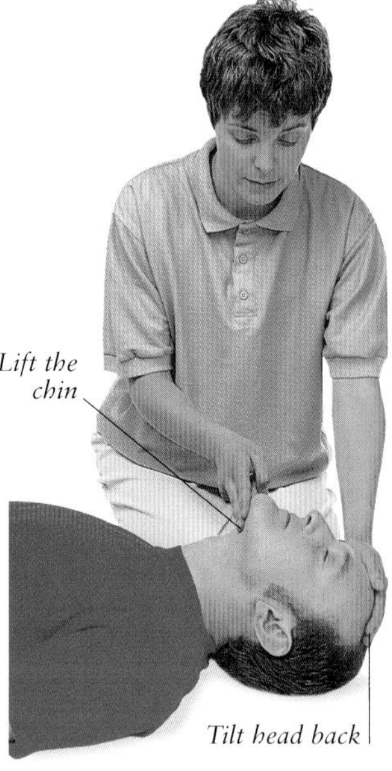

2 Remove obstructions

Remove visible obstructions from the mouth, for example, loose or badly fitting dentures.

3 Give artificial ventilation

Keeping the airway open, pinch the nose with the fingers and thumb of one hand. Take a deep breath, open your mouth and seal your lips completely over the casualty's mouth. Blow firmly and steadily until you see the chest rise, taking about two seconds for a full inflation.

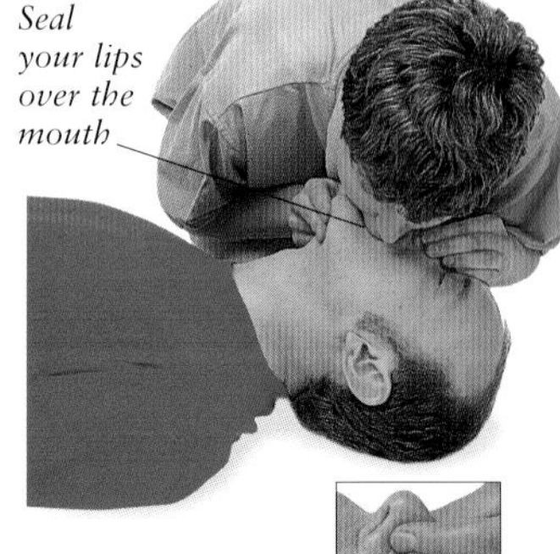

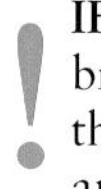

IF the casualty's chest does not move after the first breath, check that his head is far enough back and that you have closed the casualty's nose completely and then attempt ventilations again.

4 Watch the chest fall

Lift your mouth away from the casualty's mouth and turn your head towards the casualty's chest. If the artificial ventilation has been successful you will be able to see the casualty's chest falling as the air comes out of his lungs.

REPEAT STEPS 3 AND 4

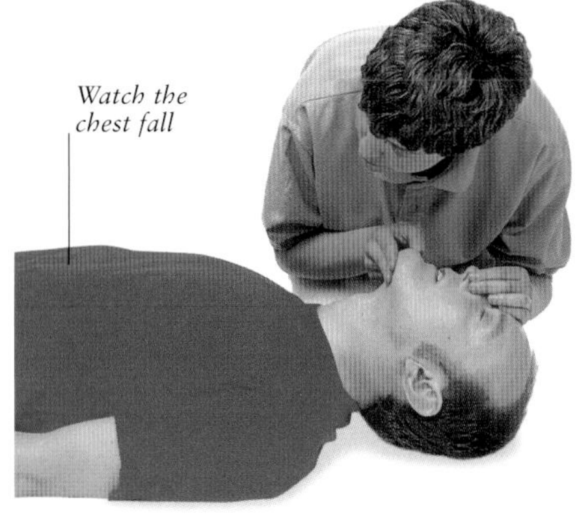

5 Check for circulation

After giving two breaths, check for the pulse in the casualty's neck (see overleaf) and for other signs of circulation such as pale skin regaining a healthy colour.

IF there is a pulse, give ten breaths of artificial ventilation in a minute.

see *The pulse* p. 15

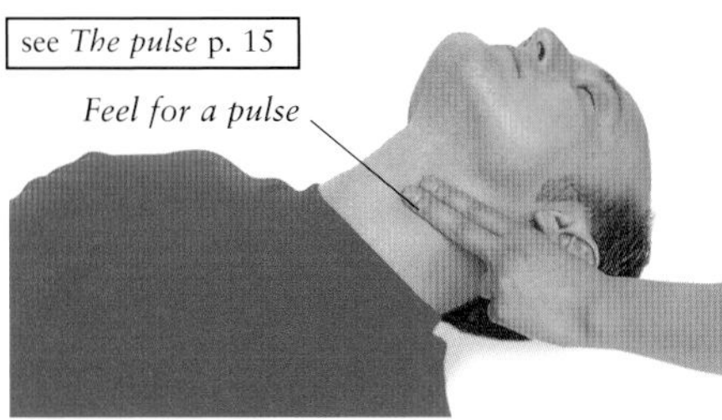

6 Continue ventilations

Continue ventilations, checking circulation after every minute.

IF circulation stops at any stage, commence CPR (see overleaf).

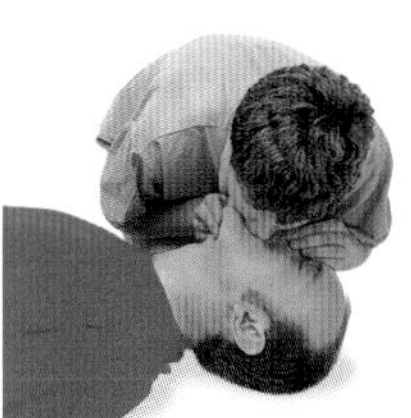

Seal the mouth; breathe into casualty

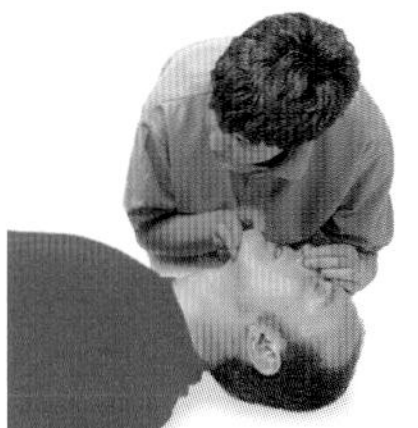

Watch the chest fall

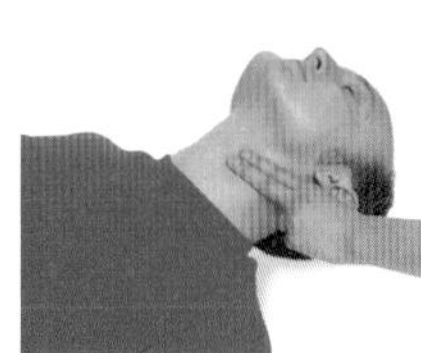

Re-check circulation every minute

see *Recovery position* p. 18

7 If breathing returns, place casualty in recovery position

If the casualty begins to breathe again, turn him into the recovery position and monitor breathing and pulse until help arrives.

Mouth-to-nose ventilation

You may blow air into the casualty's nose instead of into his mouth. To do this, make sure that the casualty's mouth is shut and then seal your lips around his nose. Give the casualty one breath and open his mouth, allowing the breath to come out.

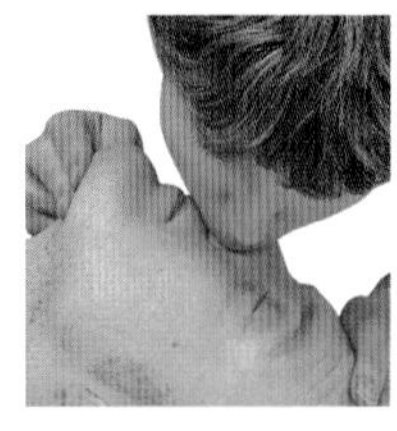

THE RESUSCITATION SEQUENCE

A quick-reference guide

Open airway

Check for breathing for 10 seconds

IF casualty is breathing, place in recovery position

IF casualty is not breathing

✚ CALL AN AMBULANCE

and continue sequence (below)

Give 2 breaths of artificial ventilation

Check the circulation (right)

IF pulse present, give ventilations for 1 minute. Re-check the circulation every minute

IF pulse absent, give CPR at rate of 15 chest compressions to 2 ventilations (right)

CHECKING CIRCULATION

Blood circulation can fail for two reasons: the heart may stop working partially, or completely (cardiac arrest) or the blood volume circulating in the body may be drastically reduced.

Check the pulse in the neck's carotid artery for ten seconds (see p. 15). Look for other signs of circulation, such as movement or return of skin colour. If circulation is not present you need to give CPR immediately (see below).

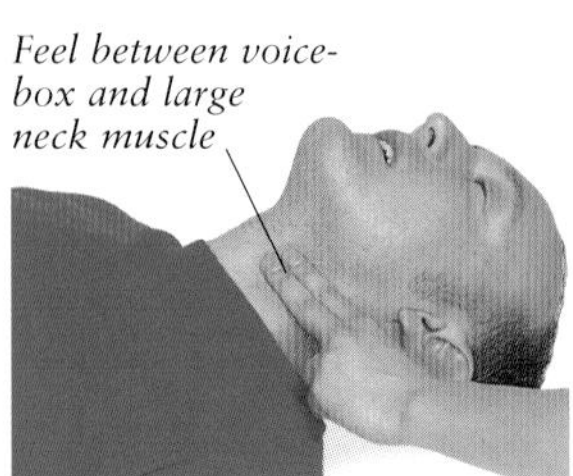

Feel between voice-box and large neck muscle

CARDIO-PULMONARY RESUSCITATION (CPR)

CPR combines chest compressions (see below) and artificial ventilations to simulate circulation. Never practise CPR on a person whose heart is beating. For children and babies, see page 25.

1 Position fingers on ribcage

Kneel on casualty's left or right side. Place the middle finger of lower hand on the point where the ribs meet and the index finger above.

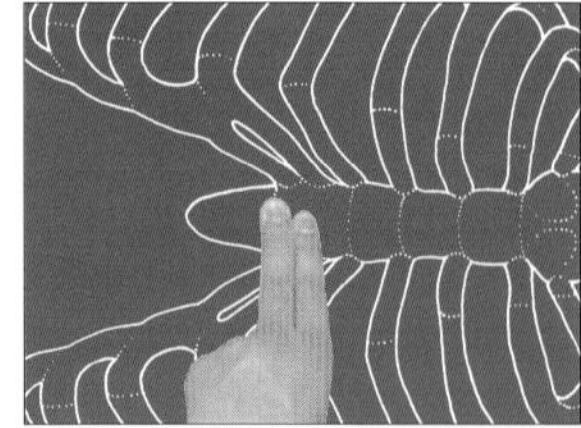

Position of fingers on the breastbone

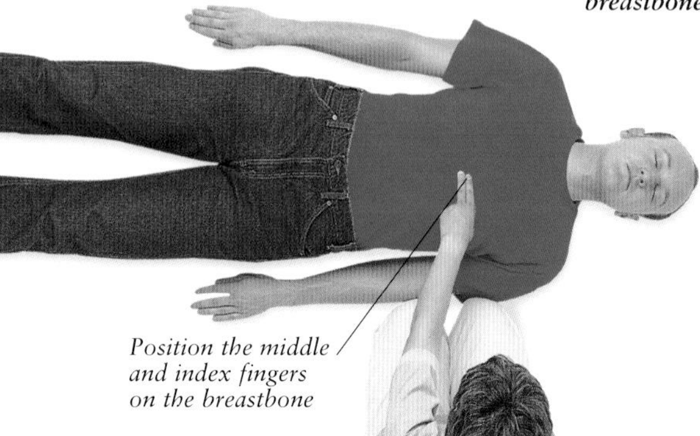

Position the middle and index fingers on the breastbone

2 Place one hand on the breastbone

Put the heel of your other hand on the breastbone next to the fingers. This is the point where you will apply pressure.

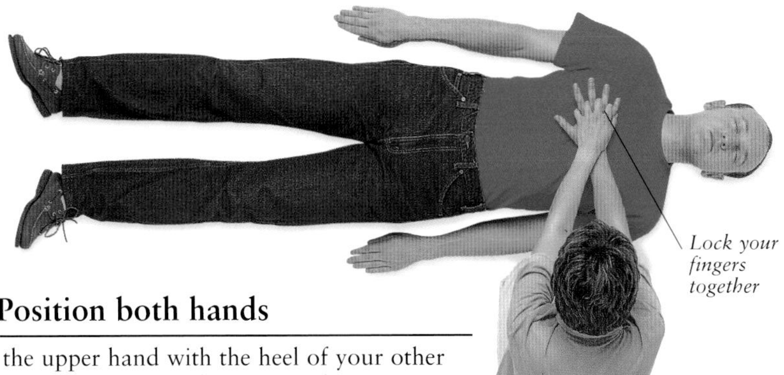

3 Position both hands

Cover the upper hand with the heel of your other hand and then lock your fingers together.

4 Kneel upright to give chest compressions

Kneel upright with your shoulders over the casualty's breastbone. Keep your arms straight. Give chest compressions; press down about 4–5 cm (1½–2 in), release the pressure, but do not remove your hands.

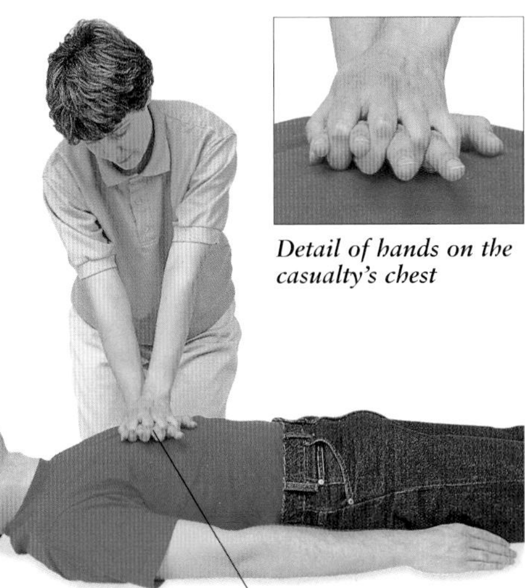

Detail of hands on the casualty's chest

5 Alternate compressions with artificial ventilations

Give 15 chest compressions; tilt the head back, lift the chin and give two breaths of artificial ventilation (see p. 20). Continue this cycle of chest compressions and breaths until help arrives.

IF there are signs of recovery, check airway, breathing and circulation again (see p. 13).

RESUSCITATION FOR A BABY OR CHILD

A quick-reference guide

Open airway

Check for breathing for 10 seconds

IF casualty is breathing, place in recovery position

IF casualty is not breathing

✚ CALL AN AMBULANCE

and continue sequence (below)

Give 5 breaths of artificial ventilation

Check the circulation

IF pulse present give ventilations for 1 minute. Re-check the circulation every minute

IF pulse absent give CPR at rate of 5 chest compressions to 1 ventilation

RESUSCITATION
FOR A BABY AND CHILD

For a child of eight or over, use the adult resuscitation sequence (see p. 16). For younger children and babies under one year, the resuscitation procedures and techniques differ slightly (see below).

1 Check for any response

For a baby: when checking a baby's response, tap the bottom of the baby's feet. Call his name, if known, to try and provoke a response.

For a child: check for a response by shaking the shoulders gently; call out the child's name, if known, to try and provoke a response. If unconscious, she will make no response.

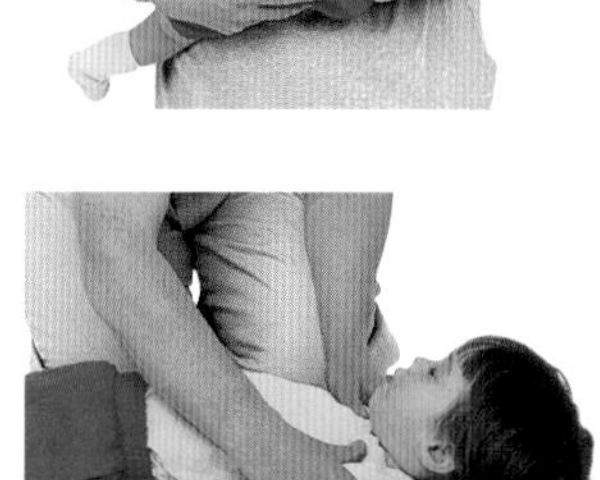

2 Open airway and check breathing

For a baby: place one finger under the chin and gently lift the chin to open the airway. Check for breathing (see p. 13).
IF breathing is present, put in the recovery position: cradle in your arms with the head tilted down (see p. 19).

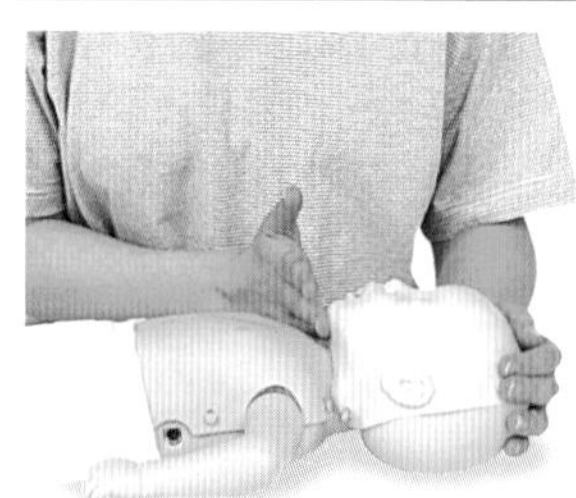

For a child: place two fingers under the child's chin and lift the chin to open the airway. Check for breathing (see p. 13).
IF breathing is present, put the child in the recovery position (see p. 19).

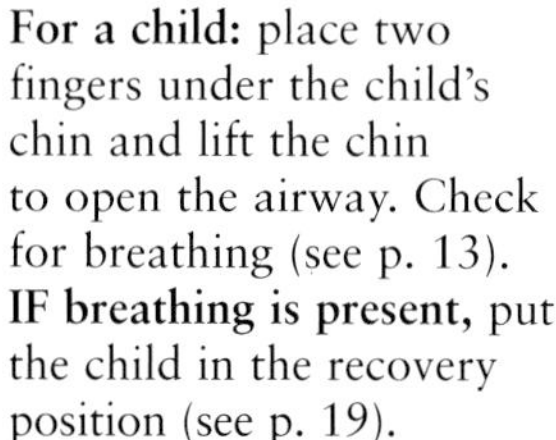

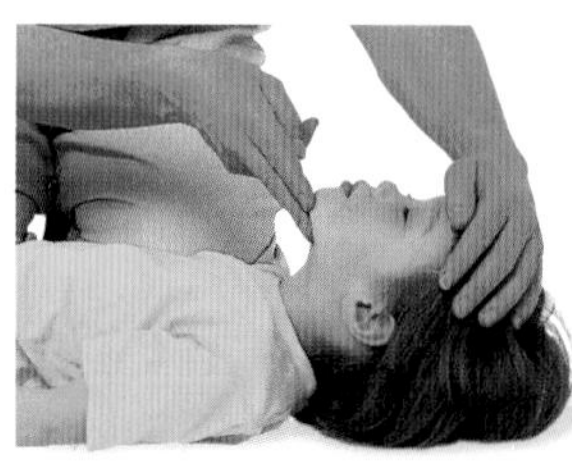

3 Give artificial ventilations

FOR A BABY

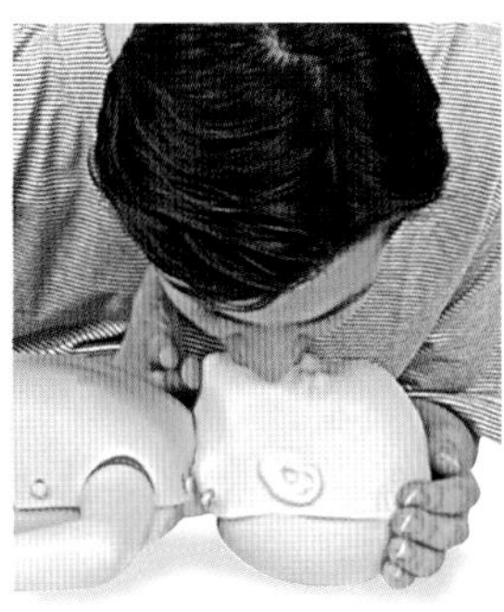

For a baby: carefully remove visible obstructions from the mouth. Lift the chin and seal the mouth and nose. Give five breaths of artificial ventilation.

For a child: treat as above but only cover the mouth, as for an adult. Give five breaths of artificial ventilation.

FOR A CHILD

4 Check for circulation

FOR A BABY

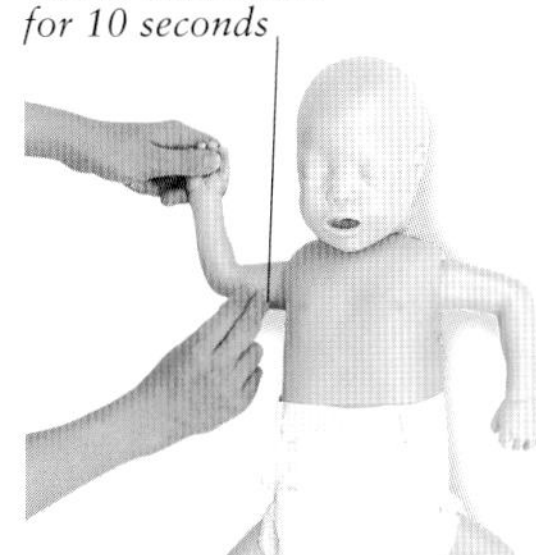

Check circulation for 10 seconds

For a baby: check the brachial pulse in the arm (see left). Continue breaths if the baby's pulse is present.
IF there is no pulse or if the pulse is less than 60, give the baby CPR (see below).

For a child: check the carotid pulse in the neck (see p. 15). If present, continue breaths. If there is no pulse, give the child CPR (see below).

FOR A CHILD

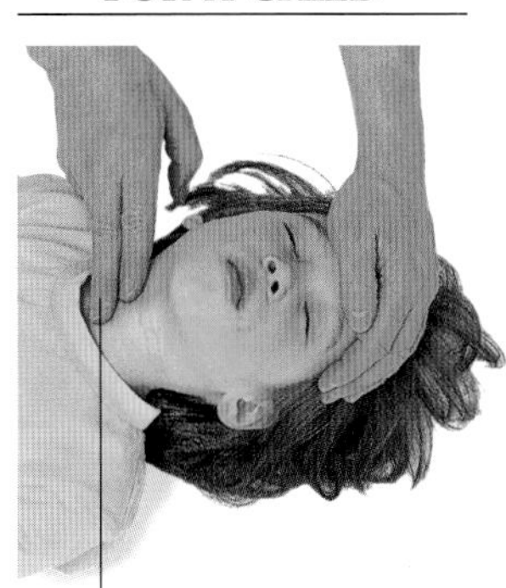

Check circulation for 10 seconds

5 Commence CPR

FOR A BABY

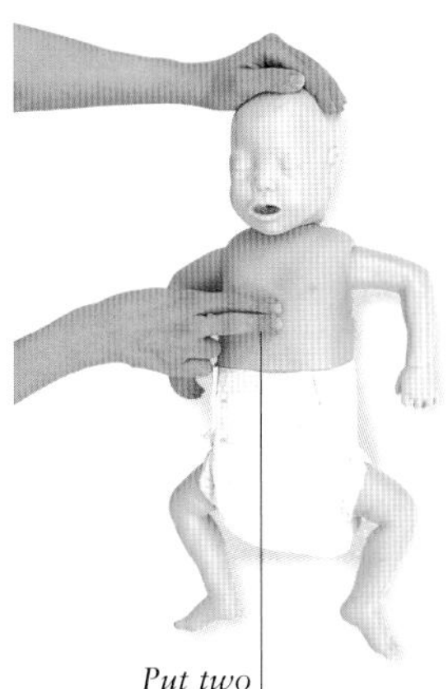

Put two fingers on the breastbone

For a baby: place two fingers on the lower breastbone. Press down five times. Give a breath of artificial ventilation.

✚ CALL AN AMBULANCE

Give CPR until help arrives.

For a child: put the heel of just one hand on the chest as for an adult (see p. 22). Press down five times. Give one breath of artificial ventilation.

✚ CALL AN AMBULANCE

Give CPR until help arrives.

FOR A CHILD

CHOKING

An object or piece of food that is stuck and blocks off the windpipe can result in choking. If the blockage remains, the casualty may lose consciousness; prompt first aid is vital. Follow the steps below and right for adults and children; see page 28 for babies.

SIGNS AND SYMPTOMS

Sudden difficulty in speaking and/or in breathing, frequently accompanied by clutching or pointing to the throat.

There may also be:

FOR AN ADULT: very reddened face.
FOR A CHILD: flushed face.
FOR A BABY: signs of distress.

FOR AN ADULT

Aim

- To clear the obstruction from the throat.
- To get the casualty to hospital, if necessary.

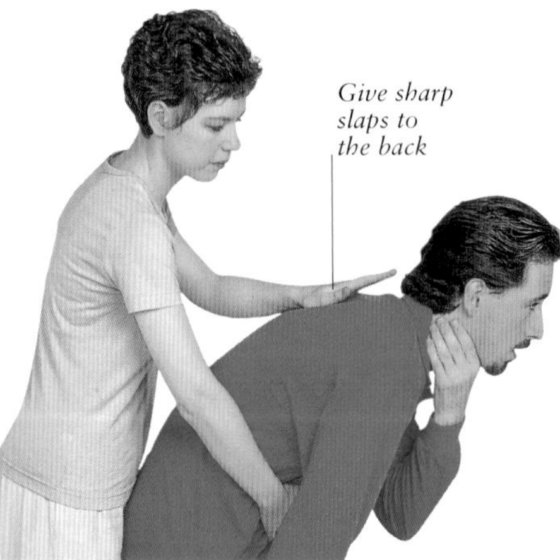

1 Give the casualty five sharp back slaps

If the casualty coughs, encourage him to continue. If he weakens or stops breathing, bend him forward. Stand behind him; give five back slaps, with the flat of your hand, between the shoulders. Check the mouth.

2 If back slaps fail, get ready to give abdominal thrusts

If the back slaps fail, stand behind the casualty and place a clenched fist with thumb side in over the upper abdomen just below the ribs.

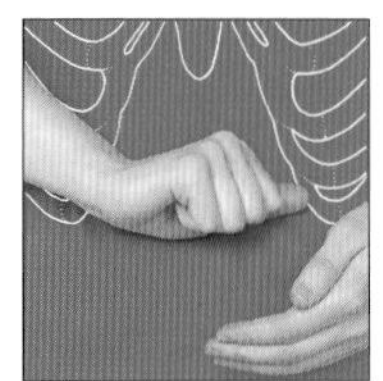

3 Give five abdominal thrusts

Grasp your fist and pull inwards and upwards, up to five times. Check the mouth.

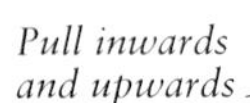

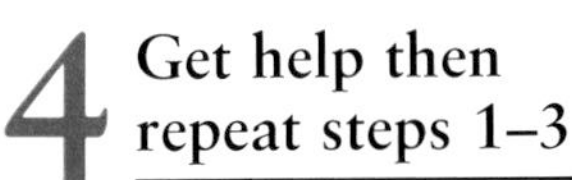

4 Get help then repeat steps 1–3

Repeat 1–3 three times. If unsuccessful,

✚ CALL AN AMBULANCE

Then continue back slaps and abdominal thrusts alternately until help arrives.

> **!** **IF** consciousness is lost, open the airway, check breathing and combine the above procedure with attempts at artificial ventilation (see p. 20).
>
> ✚ CALL AN AMBULANCE

FOR A CHILD (1–7 YEARS)

Aim

- To clear the obstruction from the throat.
- To get the casualty to hospital, if necessary.

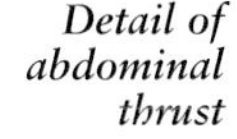

Detail of abdominal thrust

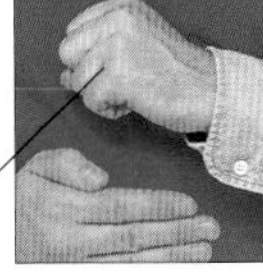

Place fist with thumb against the abdomen

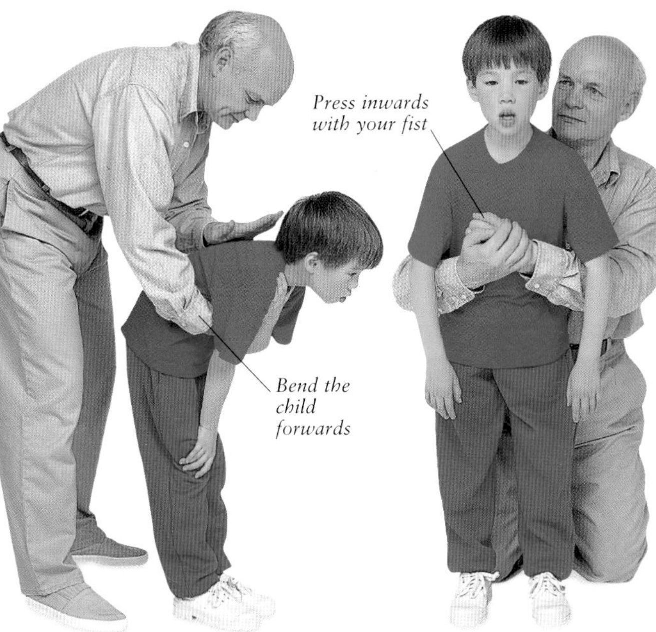

1 Give the child five back slaps

Lean the child forwards; stand or kneel behind her and give up to five back slaps between the shoulders. Look into the child's mouth and clear any visible obstructions by placing one finger in the mouth and sweeping it out.

2 Give chest thrusts

If back slaps fail, give five chest thrusts: stand behind the child, hold a fist against the breastbone and press inwards. Clear obstructions seen in the mouth.

3 Give abdominal thrusts

If the chest thrusts fail, give the child up to five abdominal thrusts: stand behind her, hold a fist against the abdomen and press sharply inwards. Check the mouth for any visible obstructions. If these fail, see step four.

4 Get help then repeat steps 1–3 three times

If, after completing steps 1–3 the blockage is still not cleared,

✚ CALL AN AMBULANCE

Continue to repeat steps 1–3 until the ambulance arrives.

> **!** IF the casualty loses consciousness, open the airway, check breathing and combine the above procedure with attempts at artificial ventilation (see p. 24).
>
> **✚ CALL AN AMBULANCE**

CHOKING (CONTINUED)

FOR A BABY (UP TO 1 YEAR)

Aim

- To clear the obstruction from the throat.
- To get the casualty to hospital, if necessary.

▶ **DO NOT** put your fingers down the baby's throat to feel for or attempt to remove an obstruction.

▶ **DO NOT** use abdominal thrusts on a baby.

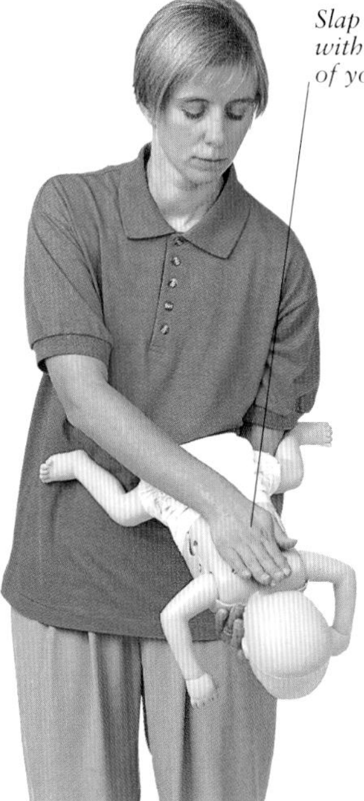

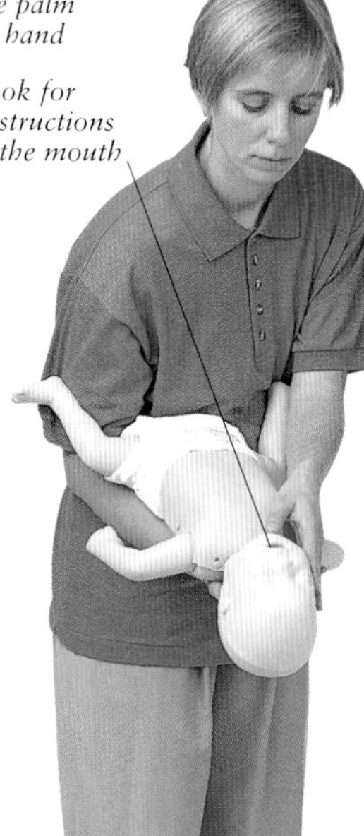

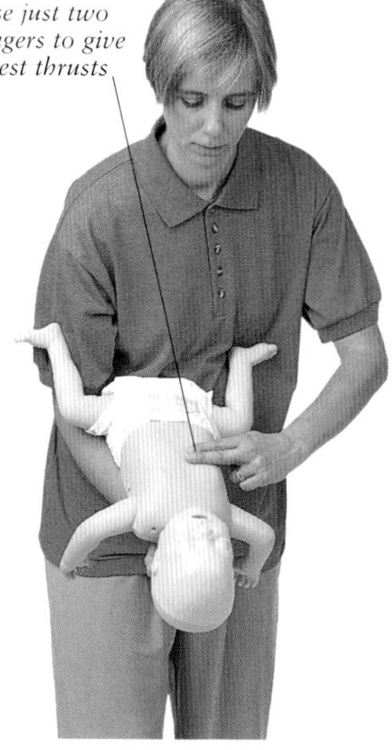

1 Give the baby back slaps

Lay the baby face down along your forearm and give up to five sharp slaps on the baby's back.

2 Remove any obstructions

Check the baby's mouth; remove any obstructions you can see by sweeping one finger into the mouth.

3 Give the baby chest thrusts

Lay the baby face up on your arm. Give up to five downwards thrusts to the chest. Check the mouth.

4 Repeat the above steps

If the obstruction has still not cleared, repeat steps 1–3 three times; keep the baby with you,

✚ CALL AN AMBULANCE

Repeat steps 1–3 until help arrives.

> ! IF, at any stage, the baby loses consciousness, open the airway, check the breathing and combine the above procedure with attempts at artificial ventilation (see p. 24). Continue this procedure until the ambulance arrives.

ASTHMA

Asthma occurs when a person's airway becomes constricted, which causes wheezing and breathing difficulties. Stimulus, such as dust, can trigger an attack, or it may occur for no apparent reason. Most sufferers use blue "reliever" inhalers to treat themselves; however, you can help to reassure the casualty, thus easing an attack.

SIGNS AND SYMPTOMS

- Breathing, especially breathing out, becomes laboured and difficult.
- Casualty may have a wheezy cough.
- Casualty becomes anxious and shows signs of distress.
- Skin on the face and the lips may have a bluish tinge.
- Casualty may become tired.
- Casualty may find it hard to talk.

Aim

- To help the casualty breathe more easily.
- To get the casualty to hospital, if necessary.

Use a blue inhaler to relieve an attack

1 Remain calm and reassure the casualty

Try to remain calm and reassure the casualty. The casualty will probably have a blue inhaler, which should relieve the attack within a few minutes.

2 Make sure the casualty is in a comfortable position

Help the casualty to relax in the position that he finds most comfortable – this will usually be in a sitting position.

- **DO NOT** ask the casualty questions that encourage him to talk unnecessarily and may increase his breathlessness.
- **DO NOT** force a casualty to lie down during an asthma attack.

IF the attack is not severe and is over within ten minutes, advise the casualty to take another dose of his inhaler.

ADVISE THE CASUALTY TO SPEAK TO A DOCTOR

IF the attack is severe and the casualty shows no signs of relief from the reliever inhaler after 10 minutes, the casualty is becoming increasingly tired or if this is the casualty's first attack,

✚ CALL AN AMBULANCE

Help the casualty to take a second breath from his blue reliever inhaler before the ambulance crew arrives. While you are waiting for the ambulance, monitor the casualty's breathing and circulation at regular intervals and reassure him.

! IF the casualty loses consciousness, open the airway, check breathing and put in the recovery position; be ready to resuscitate (see pp. 16–25).

✚ CALL AN AMBULANCE

First aid materials

You should have an easily identifiable first aid kit kept in a safe but accessible place in your home; you should also keep one in your car. The items shown below should form the basis of your kit but you may wish to add to these. Check the kit regularly and replace items that have been used or are out-of-date.

ESSENTIALS

Dressings

Small

Medium

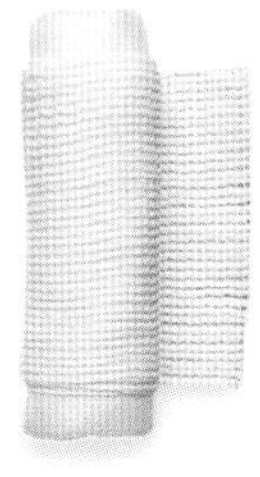

Large

Sterile dressings
These sealed dressings come in various sizes. They are placed on serious wounds to control bleeding and prevent infection.

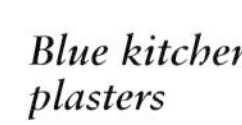

Heel and finger plasters

Blue kitchen plasters

Waterproof plasters

Clear plasters

Fabric plasters

Assorted plasters
These adhesive dressings are used to cover minor wounds to prevent infection.

Bandages

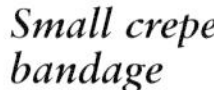

Small crepe bandage

Conforming bandages, small and large

Folded cloth bandage

Folded paper bandage

Conforming bandages
These are used to secure dressings and support injured limbs.

Triangular bandages
These are used to make slings (see p. 36) and to secure dressings (see opposite).

Securing bandages
Adhesive tapes, safety pins and clips are all useful for securing bandages. Some bandages have a clip attached.

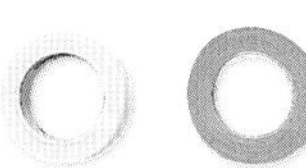

Clear and fabric tape

Safety pins and clip

Padding

Gauze pads
Sterile gauze pads can be used as padding under a bandage or as a dressing (see above).

Sterile gauze pads

USEFUL ADDITIONS

As well as the essential items, you may also wish to include a number of other items in your first aid kit. Some of these, for example, scissors and tweezers, are normal household items that prove very useful in a first aid kit. Other items, such as blankets or survival bags, should be included in outdoor camping first aid kits.

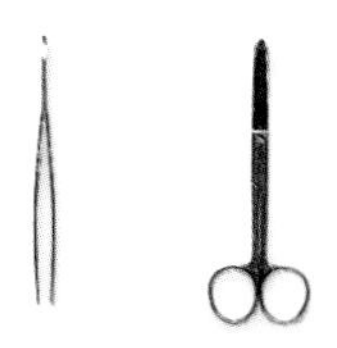

Tweezers *Scissors*

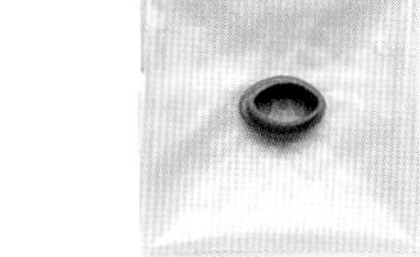

Plastic face shield

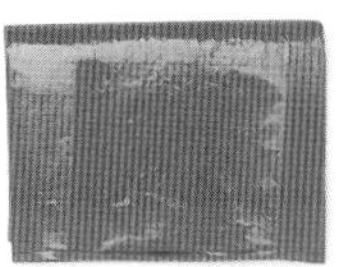

Plastic survival bag

Foil survival bag

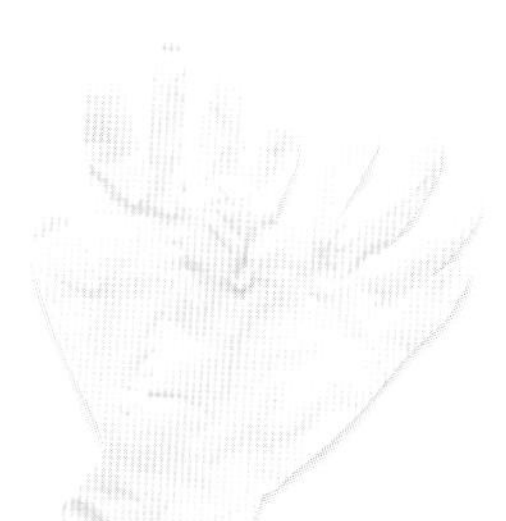

Plastic disposable gloves

Wound cleansing wipes

Notepad and pencil to record casualty's condition

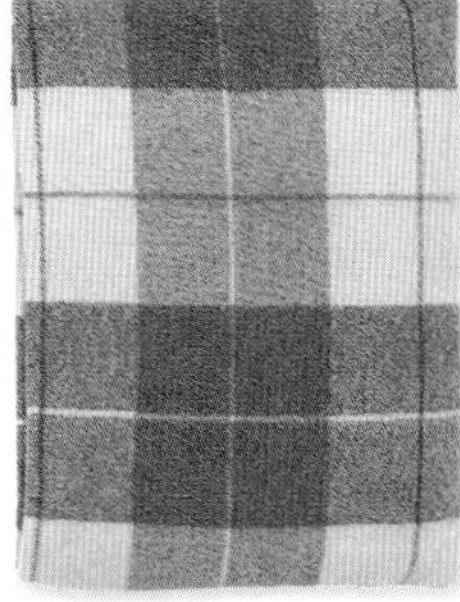

Blanket

Useful items in the car

A first aid kit in a car should be kept in a soft container to prevent anyone being injured in an accident. Extras for your car kit include:

- warning triangle to put near a road accident.
- blanket/survival bag.

Warning triangle

Broad-fold and narrow-fold bandages

These are used to secure dressings or slings (see p. 36 and p. 32).

1 Open a triangular bandage and lay it onto a flat surface.

Open triangular bandage

2 Fold the point of the triangular bandage to the base; fold the bandage in half again.

Broad-fold bandage

3 Fold a broad-fold bandage in half in the same direction.

Narrow-fold bandage

Dressings

There are several types of dressing (see below and opposite). Whatever type of dressing you choose, make sure that it is large enough to extend beyond the edges of the wound. If blood shows through a dressing, do not remove it; instead, place another dressing over it.

Sterile dressings

These absorbent gauze pads are sterilised and individually sealed in a protective wrapping. They come with or without an attached bandage (see p. 34); if without, place the pad over the injury and secure with a separate bandage.

APPLYING A STERILE DRESSING

1 Wash your hands thoroughly and unroll the short end of the bandage until the end of the dressing is visible.

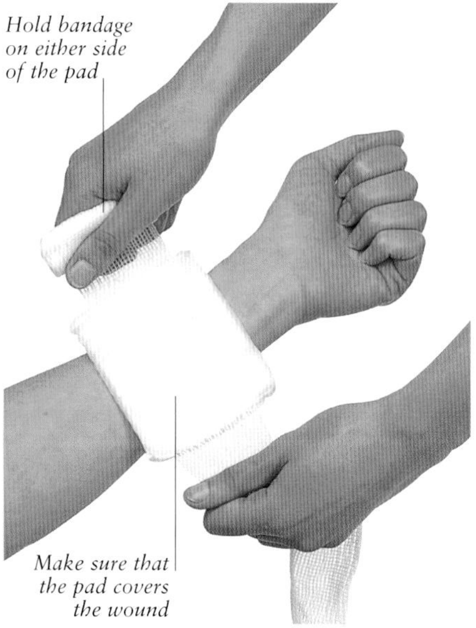
Hold bandage on either side of the pad

Make sure that the pad covers the wound

2 Open the pad next to the wound, holding the bandage over it. Place the gauze side of the pad onto the wound.

▶ **DO NOT** slide the pad onto the wound. Position it carefully over it.

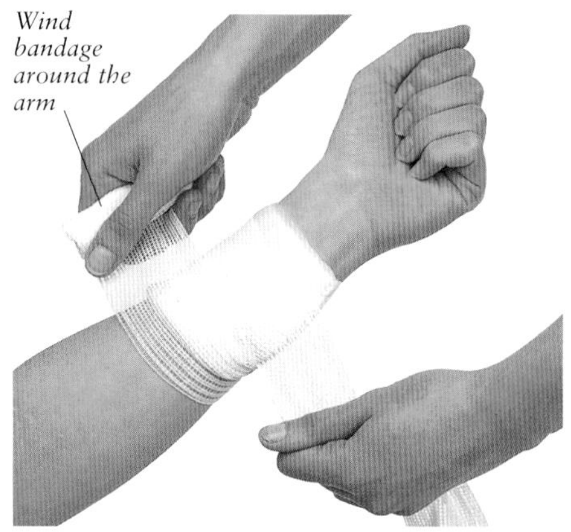
Wind bandage around the arm

3 Hold the sterile pad in place over the injury and use the long end of the roller bandage to secure it. The bandage should cover the whole of the pad.

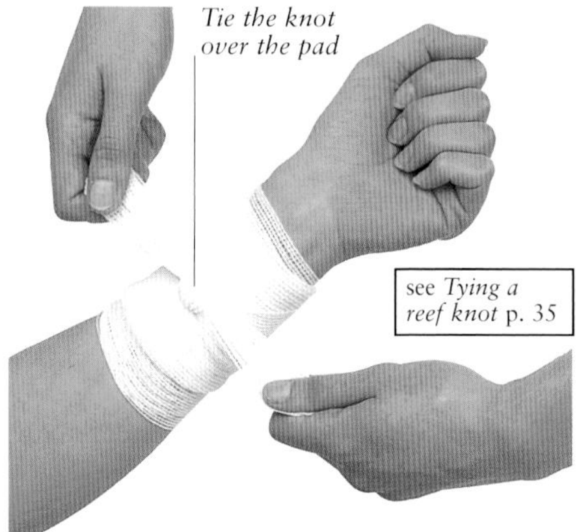
Tie the knot over the pad

see *Tying a reef knot* p. 35

4 Use a reef knot to secure the two ends of the bandage together over the pad. Check the circulation in the hand (see p. 34) and, if necessary, loosen the bandage.

PLASTERS

Available in a variety of sizes, plasters (adhesive dressings) are used to cover small cuts and grazes. Ask the casualty if he is allergic to plasters before applying one. If he is, you can use a sterile dressing.

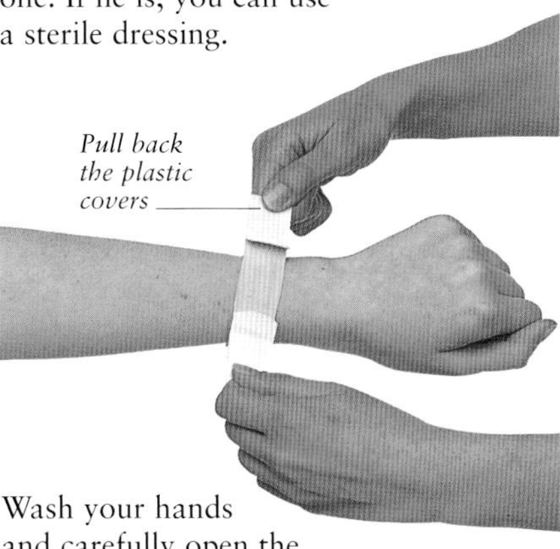

Pull back the plastic covers

Wash your hands and carefully open the sterile pack. Taking care not to touch the pad in the centre, gently pull back the plastic covers until the dressing pad is exposed. Place the dressing on the wound and pull the plastic covers further back until the plaster is secured in place.

▶ **DO NOT** leave a plaster on a cut for longer than 24 hours.

Emergency dressings

If there are no sterile dressings or plasters available, use any piece of clean, non-fluffy material to cover a wound, such as a handkerchief or pillowcase. Wash your hands, hold the material by the corners and let it fall open. Re-fold it to the size you need so that what was the inside surface is now on the outside. Handling the material by the edges only, place it over the wound and then secure the material in place with a bandage, tape or a scarf. Alternatively, if neither dressing nor material is available, you can cover the wound with a clean polythene bag.

COLD COMPRESSES

These are placed on a bruise or sprain to assist in the reduction of swelling, which in turn helps to reduce pain. Leave a cold compress on an injury for about 30 minutes. The compress can either be left uncovered over the injury or secured in place with a compression bandage. Make sure the bandage does not become too tight and affect the circulation.

MAKING A COLD PAD

1 Soak a face cloth, thin towel or similar piece of material in cold water, then wring it out until it stops dripping.

2 Fold the cloth to the required size, place it over the injury and, if possible, replace it every ten minutes, or cool it by dripping cold water onto it.

MAKING AN ICE PACK

You can make a very effective cold compress by filling a plastic bag half to two-thirds full of ice. Squeeze the air out of the plastic bag and then seal it. A bag of frozen peas or similar vegetable will also suffice. Wrap the cold compress in a thin towel and place it over the casualty's injury.

A bag of ice makes a good cold compress

CONFORMING BANDAGES

These support muscle or joint injuries, secure dressings or apply pressure to control bleeding. Made of gauze, cotton or crepe, these mould to the body's shape and keep pressure even. Once applied, check circulation: press the skin until pale; if the colour does not return, loosen the bandage.

Applying bandages

- Make sure the bandage is tightly rolled.
- Make sure the rolled part is uppermost.
- Support the part of the body in the position in which you will bandage it.
- Begin below the injury and work up the limb, from the inner side outwards.
- Always bandage from joint to joint.

SPIRAL BANDAGES

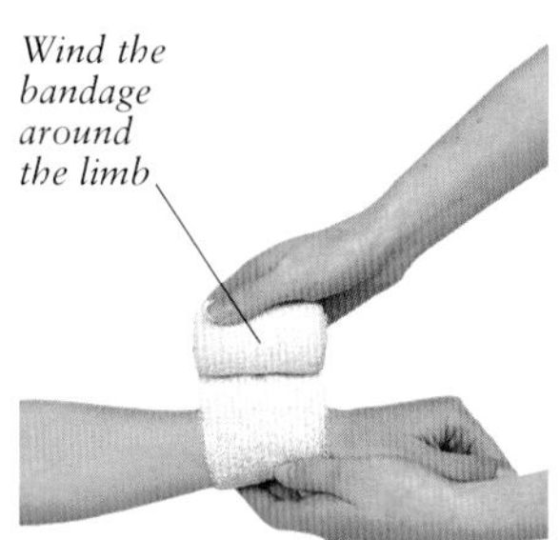

1 Place the end of the bandage on the limb and make a firm straight turn to secure the bandage.

2 Working up the casualty's injured limb, make a series of spiral turns with the bandage, allowing each successive turn to cover two thirds of the previous one.

3 Finish with a straight turn. Secure the end with either a tape or a safety pin (see right) or a bandage clip (see below), or tuck the remainder of the bandage in.

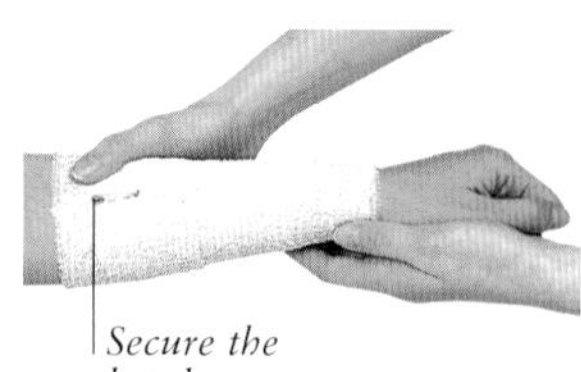

ANKLE BANDAGES

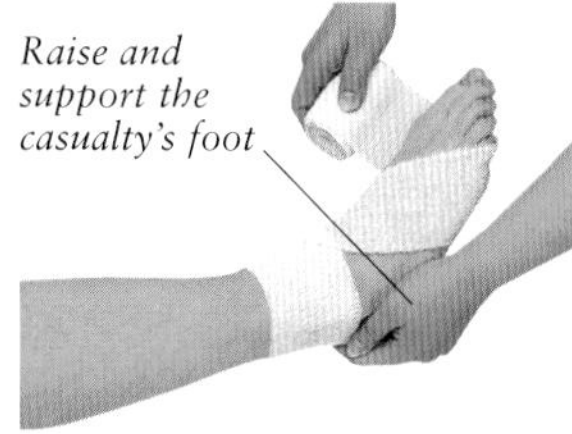

1 Wind the bandage around the ankle and take it diagonally across the foot. Bring it around the ball of the foot to the base of the big toe.

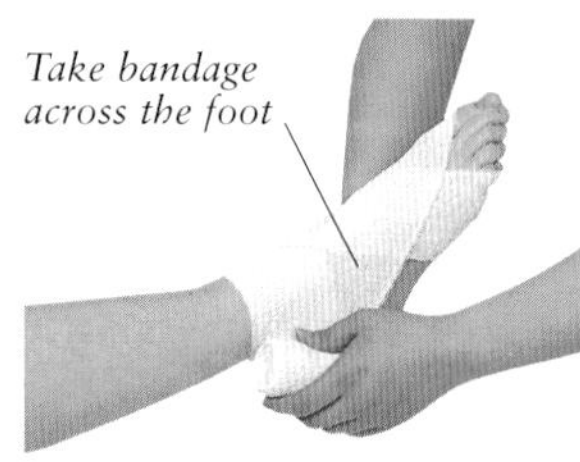

2 Pass the bandage across the top of the casualty's foot and back around the ankle. Make another straight turn around the ankle.

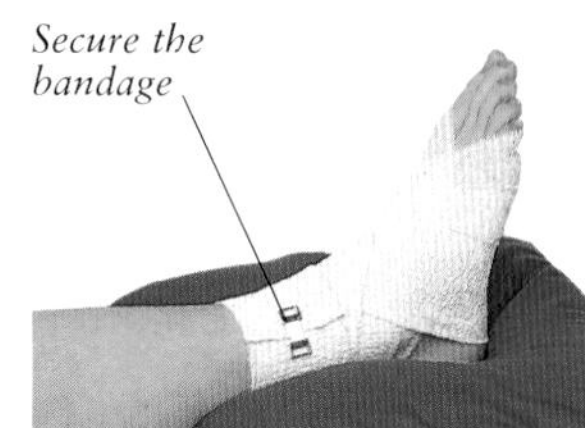

3 Continue figure of eight turns around the foot and ankle until they are covered. Make a final turn around the ankle and secure as described above.

TRIANGULAR BANDAGES

These are used to secure injured limbs, to make slings and occasionally to secure light dressings to an injury, such as a burn, where pressure does not need to be applied. They are usually made from unbleached calico or you can make one yourself using a similar piece of material about 1m square cut diagonally in half.

FOOT OR HAND BANDAGES

Use this type of bandage to hold light dressings in place, rather than to control bleeding.

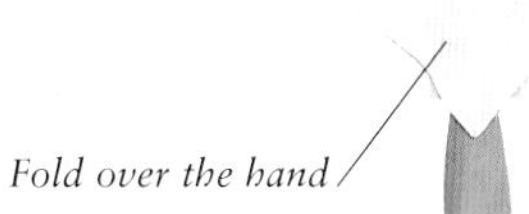

1 Place the casualty's hand on the bandage. Bring the point of the bandage over the hand onto the forearm.

2 Pass the two ends of the triangular bandage around the wrist crossing over the hand in opposite directions.

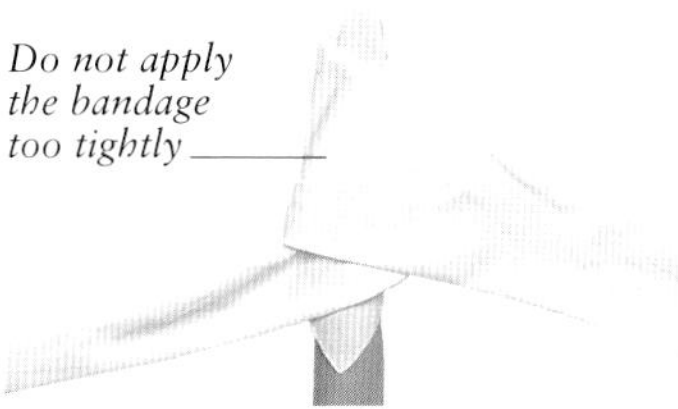

3 Tie off the two ends above the point of the bandage. Gently pull the point down to tighten and secure the bandage over the dressing.

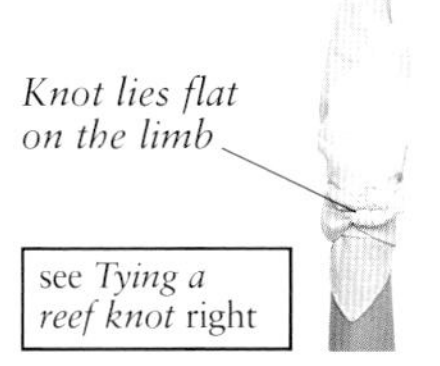

see *Tying a reef knot* right

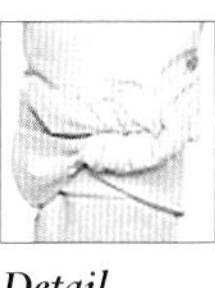

Detail of knot

4 Lift the point of the bandage over the reef knot and then tuck the point in or secure it over the reef knot with a safety pin.

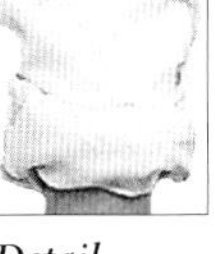

Detail of tuck

Tying a reef knot

Always use reef knots to secure a bandage because they will not slip, are comfortable because they lie flat against the casualty and are easy to undo.

1 Take one end of the bandage in each hand. Carry the right end over the left.

2 Pass what is now the left end under and through the gap.

Detail of final knot

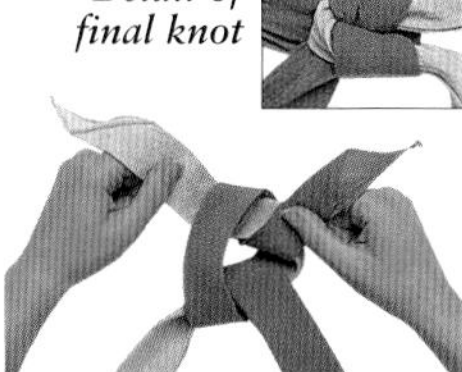

3 Carry what is now the right end over the left; pass it through the gap and pull the knot tight to secure it.

SLINGS

Arm slings support arm injuries or immobilise arms if there is a chest injury. Elevation slings raise arms to control bleeding and swelling, or are used if the collar bone, hand or rib are broken. Only use a sling if the casualty can sit or walk.

You will need

- Triangular bandage
- Safety pin

IMPORTANT

Always keep the casualty's injured arm well supported until the sling is secure and supports the arm itself.

ARM SLING

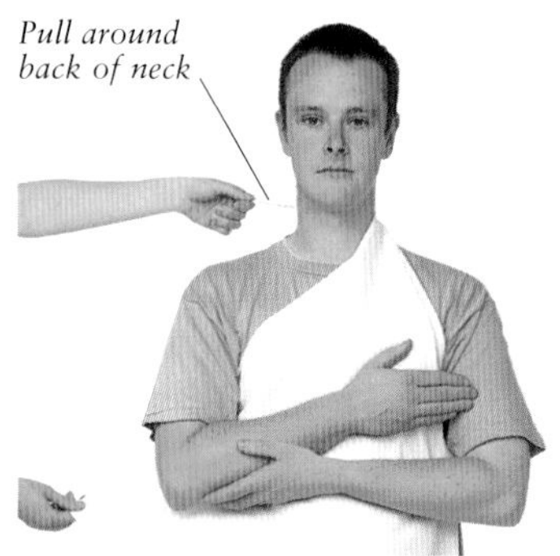

1 Sit the casualty down. Ask him to support the injured arm. Slide one end of the bandage through the hollow under the elbow. Pull the upper end until it rests by the collar bone on the injured side.

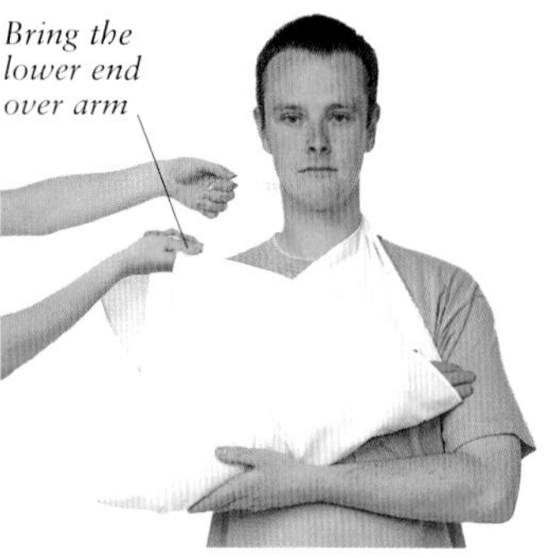

2 Bring the lower end of the bandage up over the forearm so that the injured arm is now supported by the bandage.

3 Tie a reef knot in the hollow above the collar bone on the injured side and then tuck the ends of the bandage under the reef knot.

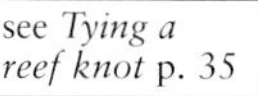
see *Tying a reef knot* p. 35

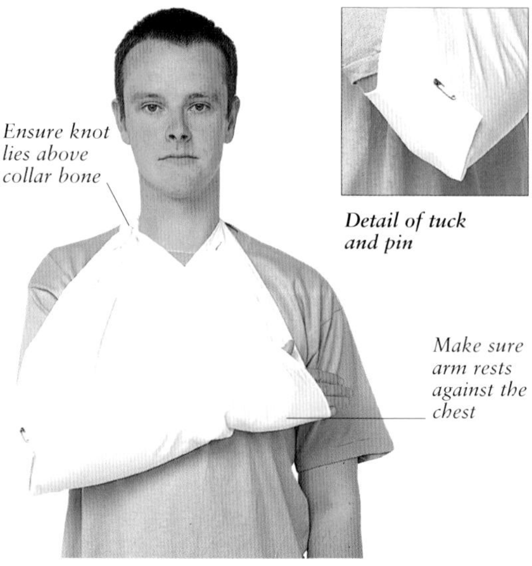

Detail of tuck and pin

4 Tuck the excess bandage behind the elbow and secure the point with either a safety pin (see above) or a twist (see opposite).

Elevation sling

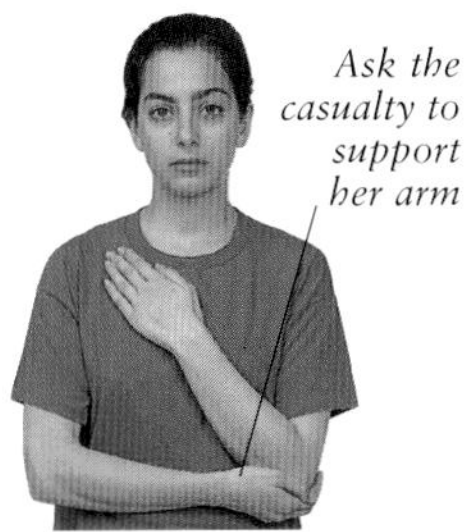

1 Support the injured arm. Place it across the chest so that the fingers reach the other shoulder.

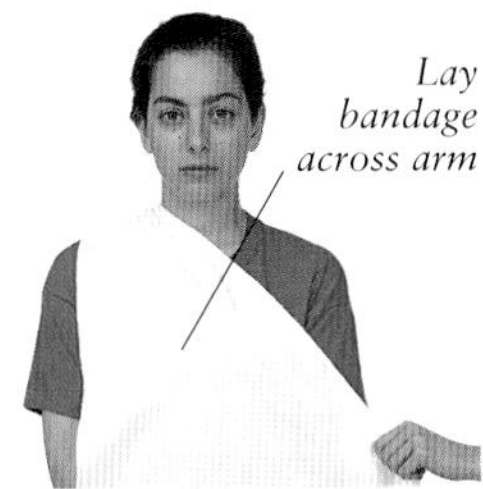

2 Lay a triangular bandage over the casualty's arm with one end over the shoulder and the point past the elbow.

3 Tuck the base of the bandage under the casualty's forearm and elbow and take the lower end of the bandage around the casualty's back and up towards the other shoulder.

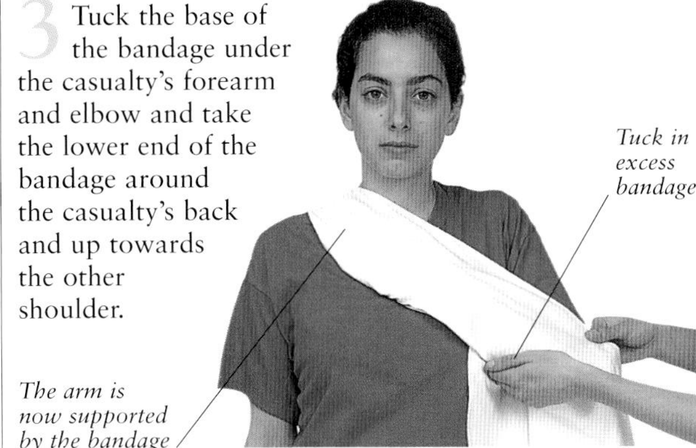

see *Tying a reef knot* p. 35

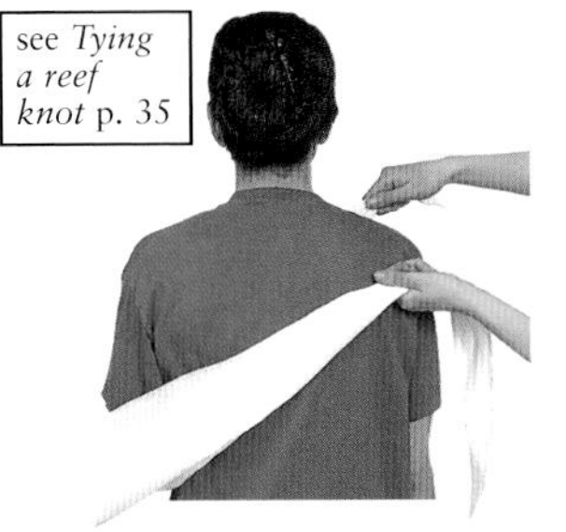

4 Tie both ends of the bandage together in the hollow above the collar bone using a reef knot.

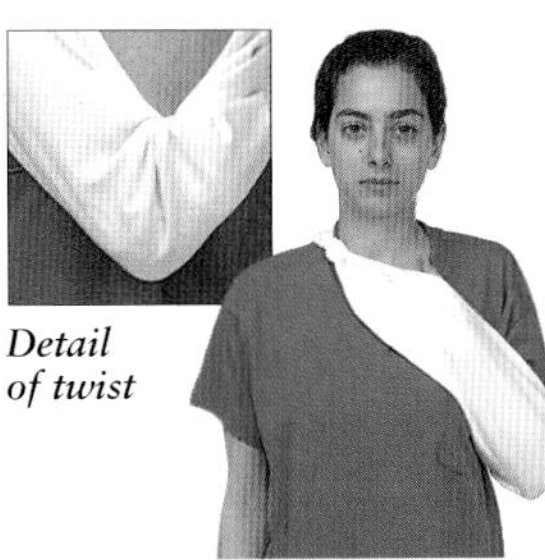

5 Tuck the point in; twist it or use a safety pin. Check the circulation in the thumb (see p. 34).

Improvised slings

Jumper
Providing the arm is not broken, support it with a turned-up jumper.

Button-up jacket
Put the arm in the fastening of a coat, or attach the cuff to the lapel with a pin.

Zip-up jacket
Turn the jacket up over the arm; attach it to the top of the jacket with a pin.

DISORDERS OF CONSCIOUSNESS

The nervous system is comprised of the brain, spinal cord and nerves. Unconsciousness occurs when a person is unable to appreciate or respond to outside stimuli. This differs from sleep because you cannot wake an unconscious person by shouting or with physical stimulus. Reflexes, such as coughing, which prevent you from choking when asleep, may also be impaired.

DEALING WITH AN UNCONSCIOUS PERSON

Once you have established that a casualty is unconscious and breathing, put him in the recovery position (see p. 18) and monitor him until help arrives.

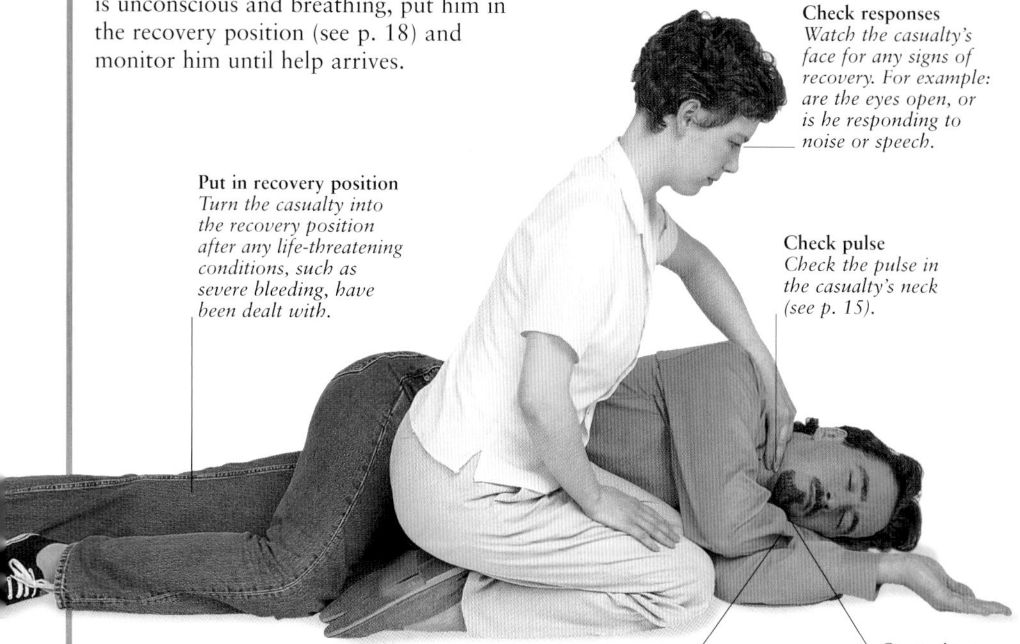

Check responses
Watch the casualty's face for any signs of recovery. For example: are the eyes open, or is he responding to noise or speech.

Put in recovery position
Turn the casualty into the recovery position after any life-threatening conditions, such as severe bleeding, have been dealt with.

Check pulse
Check the pulse in the casualty's neck (see p. 15).

Open airway
Ensure that the airway remains open and check the casualty's breathing (see p. 13).

Talisman locket

Medicalert bracelet

External signs
Look for signs such as a Medicalert bracelet or a Talisman locket (see left), worn or carried by people who suffer from conditions that may cause unconsciousness, such as epilepsy or diabetes.

CAUSES OF UNCONSCIOUSNESS

Unconsciousness may develop gradually or suddenly and it can be the result of an injury or an illness. Common causes of unconsciousness include:

- Head injury.
- Conditions that prevent blood containing oxygen getting to the brain, such as heart failure, severe bleeding, blockage in the arteries that supply blood to the brain (stroke) or fainting.
- Conditions that prevent oxygen entering the lungs, for example, chest injuries, electrical injury, blocked airway (see p. 13) or lack of oxygen in the air.
- Poisoning (see p. 80).
- Some illnesses or conditions such as epilepsy (see p. 42), hysteria (see p. 43), diabetes (see p. 41) and hypothermia or heat illness (see pp. 88–89).

LEVELS OF CONSCIOUSNESS

The casualty may pass through various levels of consciousness before unconsciousness; this may also occur as he regains consciousness. It is important to stay with the casualty all the time and record any changes in his condition. Only leave him if you have to call an ambulance and there is no-one who can call for you.

IMPORTANT

- **Maintain an open and clear airway until medical help arrives.**
- **Do not leave an unconscious casualty alone unless you have to in order to call an ambulance.**
- **Anyone who has been unconscious must be watched and seen by a doctor if recovery is not rapid and complete.**
- **Do not let the casualty eat or drink anything until he has seen a doctor.**

BEFORE TREATING AN UNCONSCIOUS CASUALTY

Look out for danger
Check for any hazards. If you are in danger do not approach the casualty.

HOW TO TREAT AN UNCONSCIOUS CASUALTY

1 Check responses and open the airway

Check the responses by talking to the casualty, gently shaking his shoulders. Tilt his head and lift the chin to open his airway (see p. 13).

2 Check for breathing

Check the casualty's breathing: put your face close to his mouth and look, listen and feel for breathing for up to ten seconds (see p. 13).

3 Turn the casualty into the recovery position

If he is breathing, treat life-threatening conditions, such as serious bleeding then put him in the recovery position (see p. 18). Check the pulse; look for other signs of circulation (see p. 15).

IF you suspect a spinal injury take extra care to keep the head and neck aligned while turning the casualty; if possible, get a bystander to help you.

✚ CALL AN AMBULANCE

4 Monitor the casualty's condition

Regularly check the breathing, pulse and responses until help arrives.

HEAD INJURIES

Any blow to the head that is heavy enough to cause a bruise or scalp wound can fracture the skull and/or result in concussion – a short period of impaired consciousness, caused by a shaking of the brain in the skull. Concussion can also result from indirect force, such as landing heavily on your feet. It is usually followed by complete recovery. If the recovery is not rapid and complete, the casualty should see a doctor as soon as possible because there may be delayed effects, such as swelling of the brain, which can cause unconsciousness to deepen.

SIGNS AND SYMPTOMS

Concussion:

- A period of unconsciousness.
- Casualty may be dazed and confused as she regains full consciousness.
- Casualty may vomit.
- Casualty may not remember the incident or anything that happened immediately before it.

If there is a skull fracture, there may be:

- Blood or blood-stained fluid coming from inside the ear or nose.
- Discoloration (bruising) around the eyelids or the white part of the eye.
- Bleeding from the scalp.
- Possible open fracture; this is particularly dangerous.

If complications develop:

- The pupils of the eyes may be enlarged or of different sizes.
- The pulse rate may be unusually slow.

FOR A CONSCIOUS CASUALTY

Aim

- To ensure that the casualty has a complete recovery.

Even if the casualty does not appear to be injured there may be a delayed reaction.

■ ADVISE THE CASUALTY TO SPEAK TO A DOCTOR

FOR AN UNCONSCIOUS CASUALTY

Aim

- To keep the airway open and resuscitate if necessary.
- To get the casualty to hospital.

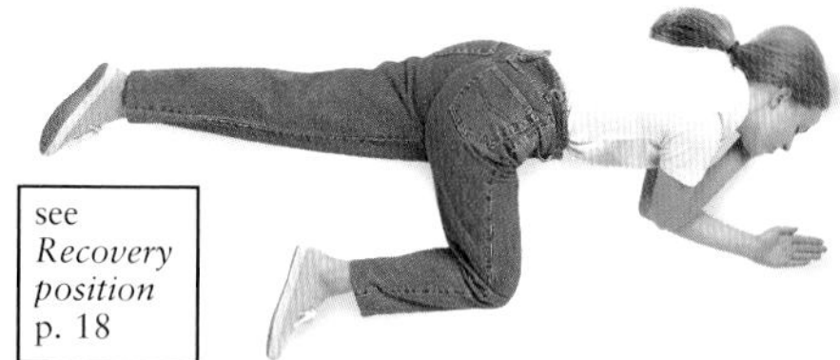

see *Recovery position* p. 18

1 Place the casualty in the recovery position

Open the casualty's airway and check the breathing (see p. 13). Place the casualty in the recovery position and ensure that the airway remains open.

2 Monitor the casualty's condition

Record breathing, pulse and responses.

IF recovery is rapid, check responses and watch for signs of deterioration.

! IF complications develop, the casualty is unconscious for more than three minutes, or is a child,

✚ CALL AN AMBULANCE

Diabetes mellitus

This condition arises when the body is unable to regulate blood-sugar levels which are normally controlled by the hormone insulin. Too much insulin can cause hypoglycaemia (see below) which, if serious, can affect consciousness. Insufficient insulin can lead to a build-up of sugar in the blood and cause hyperglycaemia (see below, right).

Hypoglycaemia

SIGNS AND SYMPTOMS

- Casualty may recognise onset of attack.
- Medic-alert bracelet/syringe/tablets.
- Sweating; cold, clammy, pale skin.
- Strong pulse and palpitations.
- Hunger, weakness and faintness.
- Confusion, low level of response.
- Shallow breathing.

FOR A CONSCIOUS CASUALTY

Aim

- To raise the blood-sugar level.
- To get medical aid.

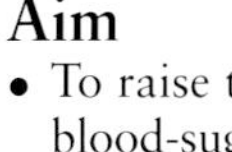

You will need

- Sugary drink

1 Give the casualty a sugary drink or sweet food

Sit the casualty down and give him a sugary drink or something sweet to eat such as a sugar lump or piece of chocolate.

2 Let the casualty rest

If the casualty improves, give him more food or drink, allow him to rest and advise him to see his doctor.

FOR AN UNCONSCIOUS CASUALTY

Aim

- To get the casualty to hospital as soon as possible.

see *Recovery position* p. 18

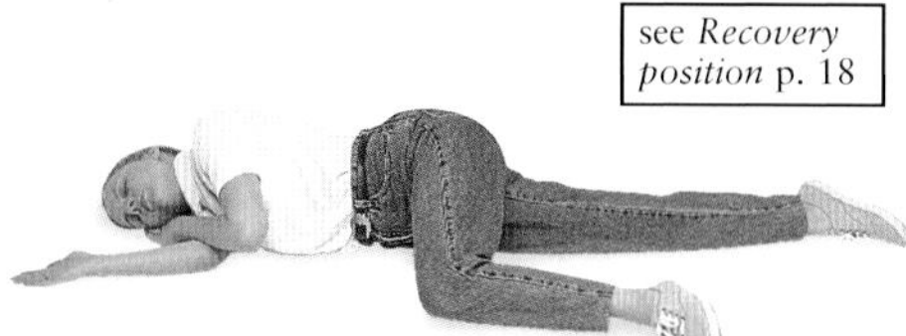

1 Place the casualty in the recovery position

Open the airway, check the breathing and place in the recovery position. Be ready to resuscitate if necessary (see pp. 16–25).

2 Monitor the casualty's condition

Monitor and record breathing, pulse and responses at regular intervals.

✚ CALL AN AMBULANCE

Hyperglycaemia

High blood-sugar levels can lead to impaired consciousness and, eventually, coma. Look for deep, heavy breathing, dry skin, rapid pulse and a smell of acetone (like nail varnish remover) on the breath. If you suspect hyperglycaemia, call an ambulance immediately.

EPILEPSY

This is a condition in which a person suffers from fits. Epilepsy is caused by a disturbance of electrical activity in the brain. These fits may be sudden and dramatic. There are two main types of fit: major or tonic/clonic fits (see below) and minor fits. Most people who are prone to epileptic fits carry warning cards or wear a Medic-alert bracelet (see p. 38). If you see a person having a major fit, try not to be frightened; act as described below. Minor fits can sometimes pass unnoticed and the person may just appear to be daydreaming.

SIGNS AND SYMPTOMS

- Sudden loss of consciousness; casualty may let out a strange cry.
- Casualty may become rigid.
- Convulsive jerking movements that may be violent.
- At the end of an attack the muscles relax and the casualty returns to normal.

Aim

- To protect the casualty from injury.
- To reassure the casualty when she recovers.

IMPORTANT

- **Never try to hold someone down or stop the convulsions.**
- **Never put anything in her mouth.**
- **Never try to give a person anything to eat or drink during a fit.**

1 Ease the fall and keep onlookers well back

If possible, try to ease the casualty's fall. Keep calm and try to stop onlookers rushing to the casualty. There is little you can do to help; let the fit run its course without interference.

2 Clear the area around the casualty

Clear a space around the casualty so that she does not hurt herself and protect her from any danger. If possible, place some soft padding under or around her head.

Loosen tight clothing

Place something soft under her head

3 Loosen tight clothing

If possible, loosen any tight clothing on the casualty and protect her head. Do this very carefully as it is easy to frighten a semi-conscious person.

see *Recovery position* p. 18

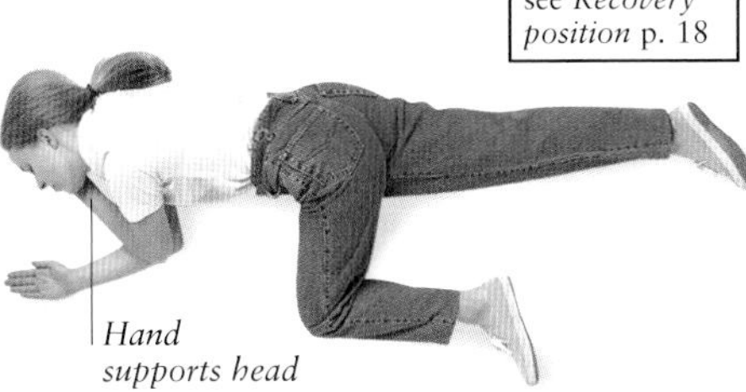

Hand supports head

4 Place the casualty in the recovery position

When the jerking stops, open the airway, check the breathing and turn the casualty into the recovery position.

5 Remain with the casualty and reassure her

When the attack is over, remain with the casualty until you are sure that she has completely recovered and can get home.

> ! **IF** the fit lasts more than five minutes, unconsciousness more than 10 minutes, if consciousness is not regained between fits or if this is the person's first fit,
>
> ✚ CALL AN AMBULANCE

Give casualty space so that she does not hurt herself

HYSTERIA

True hysteria is caused by psychological stress, which in turn can lead to an actual physical complaint. At the scene of an accident, a person may behave "hysterically" and appear to be over-reacting; he or she should be treated kindly but firmly.

SIGNS AND SYMPTOMS

- Strange behaviour; the casualty may wave her arms and legs about.
- The casualty may shout and scream, or go into a trance-like state.

Aim

- To try to calm the casualty.

1 Comfort and reassure the casualty

Reassure the casualty; be understanding and firm. Ask onlookers to move away; an hysteric will play up to an audience.

2 Advise the casualty to visit her doctor

When the casualty has calmed down, advise her to see a doctor.

> ! **IF** you are unsure about the casualty's condition, or if she is unconscious, place her in the recovery position.

see *Recovery position* p. 18

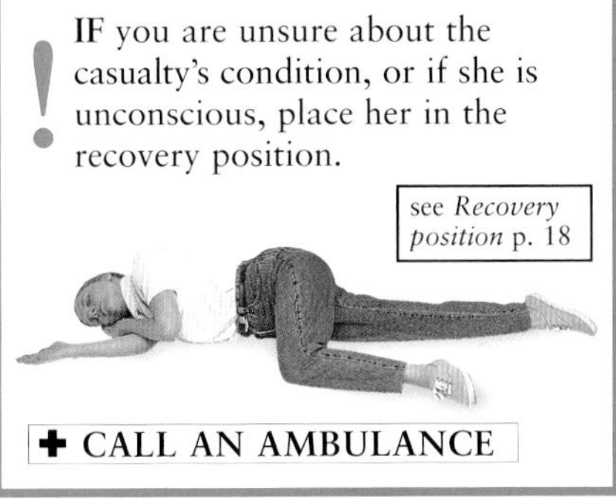

> ✚ CALL AN AMBULANCE

Convulsions in children

These occur mainly in young children between the ages of one and four and are generally caused by a very high temperature (fever), serious tummy upset, fright or temper. Although convulsions can look very alarming, they are not usually dangerous and problems rarely occur afterwards.

SIGNS AND SYMPTOMS

- The child may be flushed and sweating with a very hot forehead.
- The back may stiffen and arch.
- Eyes may be rolled upwards.
- The child may hold her breath causing her face to have a bluish tinge.
- Consciousness may be briefly lost.

Aim

- To prevent the child's temperature from rising further.
- To protect the child from injury.

You will need

- Padding
- Tepid water
- Sponge

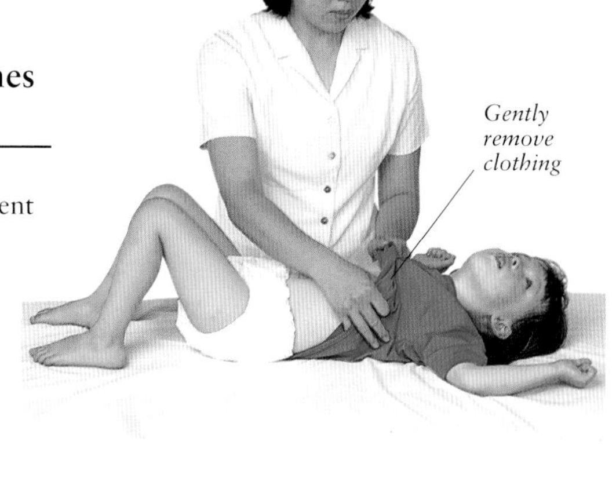

Gently remove clothing

1 Remove the child's clothes and any bedclothes

Remove the child's clothing and any bedclothes covering the child to prevent her temperature from rising further.

2 Clear the immediate area around the child

Clear a space around the child. Wipe away froth from around her mouth.

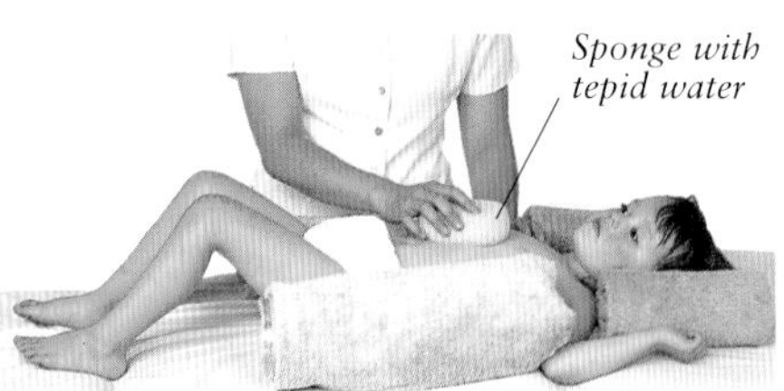

Sponge with tepid water

Put a sheet over the child

3 Place soft padding around the child and cool her

Place towels or pillows around the child to prevent her from injuring herself by a sudden movement. Cool the child by sponging her down with tepid water; work from the head downwards.

IF possible, encourage the child to lie on her side when the convulsions stop.

IF the child briefly loses consciousness, put her in the recovery position (see p. 19). Cover her with a sheet and reassure her.

☎ CALL A DOCTOR

FAINTING

This is a short loss of consciousness that occurs when the bloodflow to the brain is temporarily reduced. Fainting can be caused by emotion and, most commonly, by pain. It can also occur if someone stands for a long time in a hot atmosphere; moving the feet and/or changing position can prevent this. Recovery is usually rapid and complete once the appropriate action is taken (see below).

SIGNS AND SYMPTOMS

- The casualty will feel weak, faint, giddy and possibly nauseous.
- Very pale skin.
- Slow pulse.
- Loss of consciousness.

Aim

- To make sure blood reaches the casualty's brain.
- To make the casualty comfortable.
- To reassure the casualty after recovery.

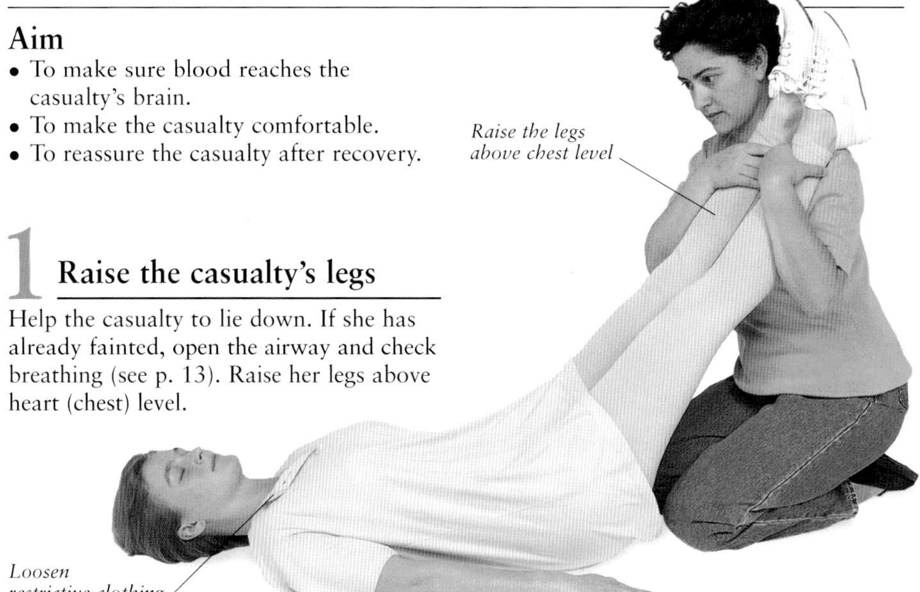
Raise the legs above chest level

Loosen restrictive clothing

1 Raise the casualty's legs

Help the casualty to lie down. If she has already fainted, open the airway and check breathing (see p. 13). Raise her legs above heart (chest) level.

2 Make sure the casualty has plenty of fresh air

Loosen tight clothing around the neck, chest and waist. Open any windows and ask bystanders not to crowd the casualty.

3 Reassure the casualty and treat any injuries

Once the casualty starts to recover, reassure her constantly and help her to slowly sit up. Look for any other injuries and treat these accordingly.

! **IF** the casualty does not regain consciousness after three minutes, put her in the recovery position.

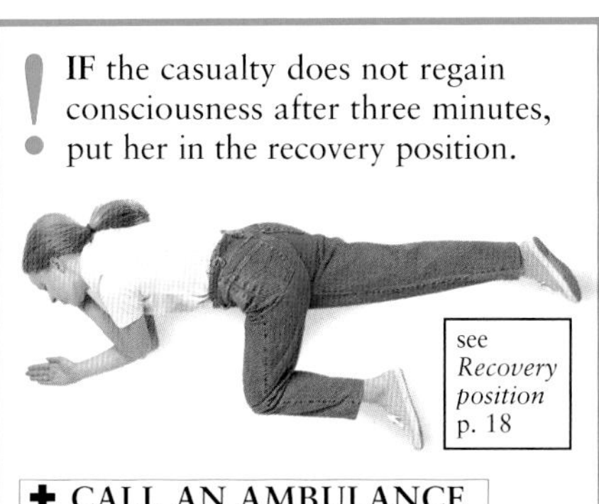

see *Recovery position* p. 18

✚ CALL AN AMBULANCE

STROKE

A stroke occurs when the blood supply to part of the brain is interrupted by a blood clot or a damaged blood vessel. Strokes usually occur in elderly people and can either be minor, when a full recovery is possible, or major and possibly fatal. The severity of a stroke depends on how much of the brain has been affected.

SIGNS AND SYMPTOMS

The following may occur:

- ▶ A severe, sudden headache.
- ▶ Dizziness and confusion.
- ▶ Casualty may lose consciousness; this may be gradual or sudden.
- ▶ Casualty may show signs of paralysis on one side of the body, for example, he or she may have impaired vision or experience difficulty in speaking.

FOR A CONSCIOUS CASUALTY

Aim

- To keep the casualty comfortable.

You will need

- Flannel

1 Support the casualty's head and shoulders

Lay the casualty down, making sure that her head and shoulders are slightly raised.

2 Tilt the head to one side

Tilt the casualty's head to one side. Wipe her face with a flannel if she dribbles.

▶ **DO NOT** allow the casualty to have anything to eat or drink.

✚ CALL AN AMBULANCE

FOR AN UNCONSCIOUS CASUALTY

Aim

- To make sure that the casualty's airway remains open.
- To arrange for the casualty to be taken to hosptial.

1 Open the airway and check the breathing

Open the casualty's airway, check the breathing and be ready to resuscitate if necessary (see pp. 16–25).

see *Recovery position* p. 18

2 Place in recovery position

Place the casualty in the recovery position. Ensure that the airway remains open.

3 Monitor the casualty's condition

Monitor and record breathing, pulse and responses at regular intervals.

✚ CALL AN AMBULANCE

Heart attack

A heart attack usually occurs when the blood supply to part of the heart muscle becomes blocked by a blood clot in one of the coronary arteries. The severity of the attack depends on the extent of muscle damage. If you suspect that a casualty has suffered a heart attack, arrange for him to be taken to hospital as soon as possible.

SIGNS AND SYMPTOMS

- Severe, crushing pain in the centre of the chest that may radiate down the casualty's left arm.
- Breathlessness, faintness and nausea.
- Pale, cold and clammy skin.
- Pulse is rapid, weak or irregular.
- Casualty may feel a sense of impending doom.
- Casualty may collapse suddenly.

Aim

- To minimise the work of the heart.
- To get the casualty to hospital as soon as possible.

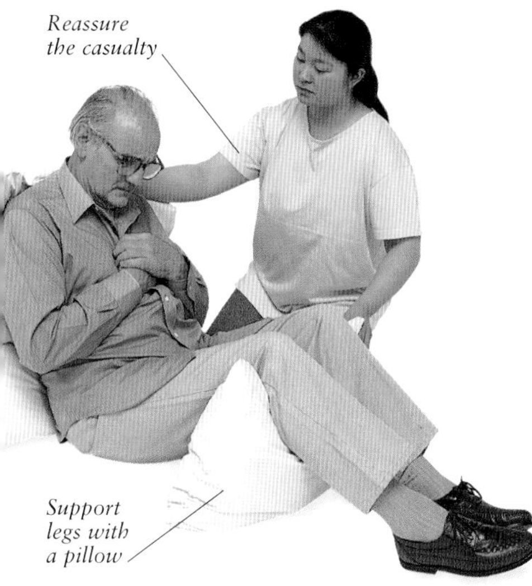

1 Place the casualty in a comfortable position

Help the casualty to rest in a comfortable position to lessen the strain on his heart. Ideally, this should be a sitting position with the back and shoulders supported and the knees bent and supported.

✚ CALL AN AMBULANCE

2 Monitor the casualty's condition

Monitor the casualty's breathing and pulse and be ready to resuscitate the casualty if necessary (see pp. 16–25).

IF the pain continues and the casualty is completely conscious, give him an aspirin to chew slowly.

Blood clot in the heart

A heart attack occurs when a blood clot forms inside a diseased or narrowed coronary artery, depriving surrounding heart muscle of oxygen which, in turn, causes the affected heart muscle to die.

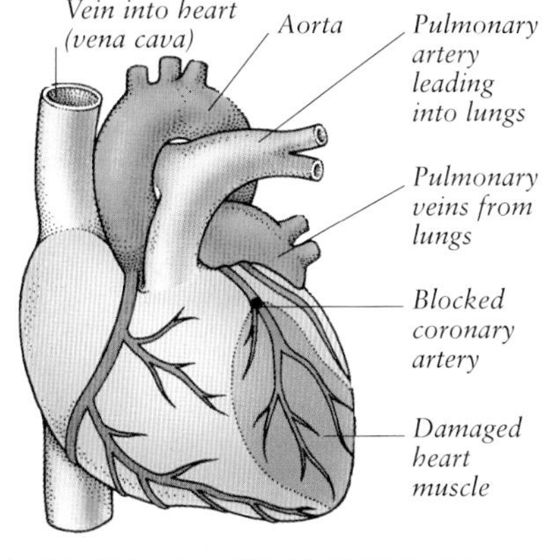

WOUNDS AND BLEEDING

A wound is an injury that breaks the skin and allows blood to escape and germs to enter. A severe bleed is serious and must be controlled immediately. If a large amount of blood is lost, shock (see p. 51) and eventually death may occur.

DEALING WITH SEVERE BLEEDING

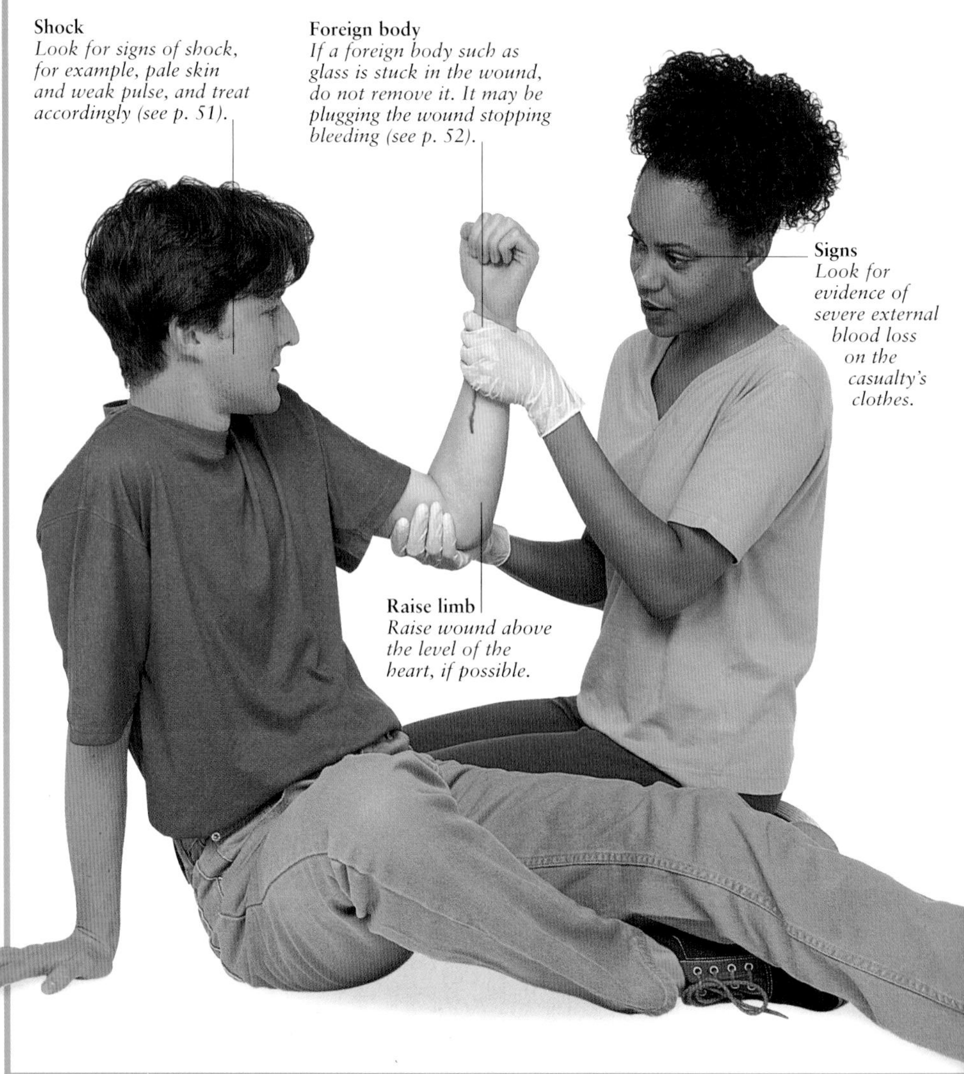

TYPES OF BLEEDING

Bleeding occurs when any of the blood vessels are cut or torn; it may be external, that is visible, or internal. External bleeding is categorised by the type of vessel that is damaged.

There are three types of bleeding:

Arterial bleeding
Arteries carry oxygenated blood from the heart around the body. Blood from an artery is bright red and spurts from a wound in time with the heart beat.

Venous bleeding
Veins carry deoxygenated blood from around the body back to the heart. Blood from a vein is a darker red and pours from a wound.

Capillary bleeding
These small blood vessels link arteries and veins. If a capillary is damaged, blood will ooze from the wound. This is the most common type of wound.

BEFORE YOU TREAT BLEEDING

- **Look out for danger**
  Check for any hazards. If you are in danger, do not approach the casualty.

- **Follow the ABC** see *Resuscitation* pp. 16–25
  If the casualty appears unconscious check his responses; if unconscious, open the airway and check breathing; if breathing, put the casualty into the recovery position. Check the circulation and keep the casualty's airway open. Be ready to resuscitate the casualty if necessary.

HOW TO TREAT BLEEDING

1 Examine the wound

Examine the wound and check for any foreign bodies.

2 Apply direct pressure to the wound

Press on the wound, preferably over a clean pad, to help the blood to clot. Apply pressure either side of the wound if there is a foreign body (see p. 52).

3 Raise and support the limb

If the casualty is bleeding from a limb, raise and support the limb above the level of the heart.

4 Place a sterile dressing over the wound

Secure a dressing or clean non-fluffy material over the wound. Put extra dressings on if blood shows through.

5 Check for shock

Watch for any signs of shock and, if necessary, treat the casualty for shock (see p. 51).

☐ TAKE OR SEND THE CASUALTY TO HOSPITAL

Blood vessels and bleeding

The main component of blood is a fluid called plasma that contains red and white blood cells. Blood also contains platelets, which are small cells that help the blood to clot. Blood is transported around the body by vessels called arteries, veins and capillaries (see right). If blood vessels are damaged, they contract at the site of the injury and the blood-clotting process, below, is activated.

Arteries
These have muscular walls through which blood travels at high pressure. Arteries pump blood with oxygen from the heart to the tissues.

Capillaries
These tiny vessels connect arteries and veins. Their thin walls allow oxygen and nutrients to pass to the body tissues.

Veins
Blood without oxygen is carried back to the heart via the veins that have thinner, less muscular walls than the arteries.

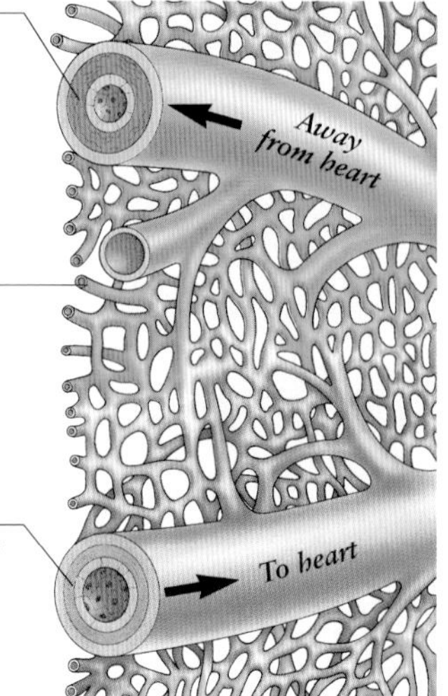

Blood-clotting

A blood clot is the solidification of blood occurring either spontaneously within a blood vessel or as the result of a leakage outside the vessel. A clot that forms outside a blood vessel usually occurs in response to damage to the vessel. For example, at a wound, blood leaks from the skin because the blood vessels are damaged and then solidifes to form a clot (see below). At the same time the blood vessels constrict to limit the blood flow from the site of the wound.

How blood clots

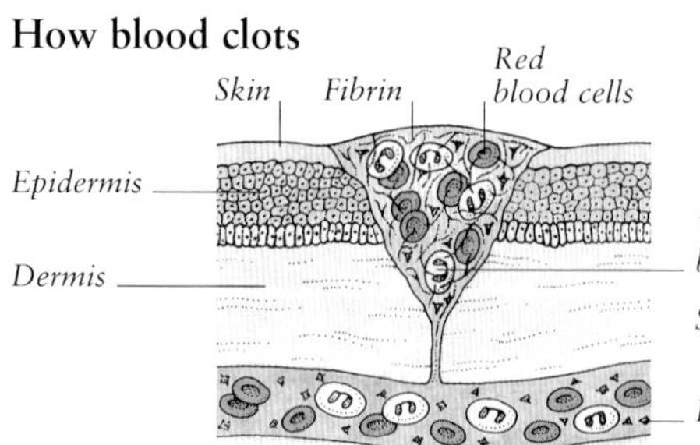

1 Small blood cells, called platelets, clump together at the site of the wound. The platelets and damaged blood vessels react to form a chemical called thrombin which, in turn, reacts with a blood protein and creates fibrin filaments to form a mesh at the wound site.

2 More platelets and red and white blood cells gather together inside the fibrin mesh. The fibrin filaments then contract and a clot is quickly formed. Eventually, the clot hardens and a protective scab forms over the site of the cut, which then heals leaving a scar.

SHOCK

This condition occurs when the circulation fails because the heart weakens, for example, if the blood supply is reduced by bleeding or fluid loss due to burns, vomiting or diarrhoea. It can also occur during anaphylactic shock (see p. 83). This reduction in circulating fluids limits the brain's oxygen supply.

SIGNS AND SYMPTOMS

- Pale, cold and clammy skin.
- Casualty may experience nausea.
- Pulse is rapid and then weak.
- Fast and shallow breathing.
- Casualty is restless, yawns and sighs.
- Casualty may be thirsty.
- Gradual loss of consciousness; eventual death if treatment is not successful.

Aim

- To treat any obvious causes of shock.
- To improve circulation.
- To get the casualty to hospital.

You will need

- Blanket

Internal bleeding

This can result from damage to an internal organ or from an injury that causes a major bone, such as a thigh bone (femur) or pelvis, to break; both of these conditions can cause severe bleeding inside the body cavities.

You should suspect internal bleeding if the casualty is displaying signs of shock, if you notice a large amount of swelling around the site of the injury, or if the casualty is experiencing a marked degree of tenderness around the abdomen.

1 Treat any injuries

Treat any obvious injuries, such as bleeding, burns or broken bones.

2 Gently raise the legs and reassure the casualty

Lie the casualty down. Raise his legs if they are not injured. Reassure the casualty.

3 Cover the casualty to keep him warm

Protect the casualty from extremes of temperature, if necessary placing a blanket or coat around him to keep him warm.

Record the casualty's responses

✚ CALL AN AMBULANCE

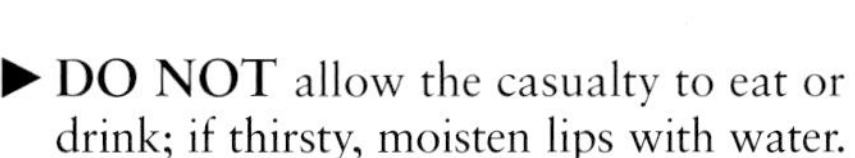

4 Monitor the casualty's condition

Check the casualty's breathing, pulse and level of response at regular intervals.

▶ **DO NOT** allow the casualty to eat or drink; if thirsty, moisten lips with water.

EMBEDDED OBJECT

If there is an object embedded or stuck in a wound, never remove it: first, because it may be plugging the wound preventing bleeding and second, because you may do more damage by pulling it out. Instead, protect the area with gauze and place a dressing made of spare rolled-up bandages around the object, held in place with another bandage. This will maintain enough pressure to control the bleeding without pressing directly on the wound or the object.

Aim

- To control bleeding.
- To protect the wound from infection.
- To immobilise the affected area.

You will need

- Disposable gloves
- Piece of gauze
- Bandages for padding and to cover wound
- Safety pin

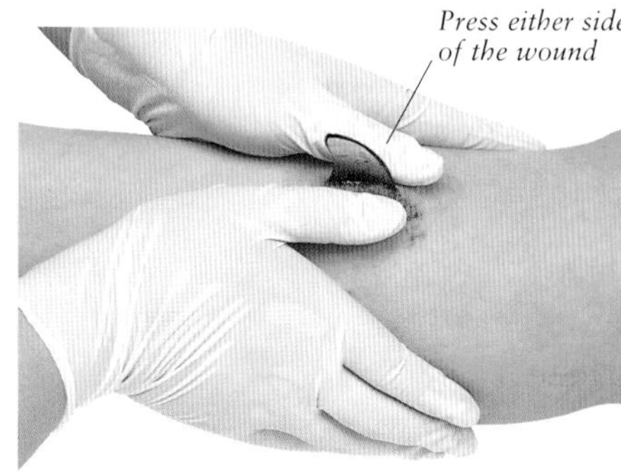

Press either side of the wound

1 Pinch the edges of the wound together

Apply pressure to control severe bleeding by pinching the edges of the wound together around the embedded object.

2 Raise and support the injured part

Help the casualty to lie down and, if possible, raise and support the injured part. Drape a piece of gauze over the wound and the protruding object.

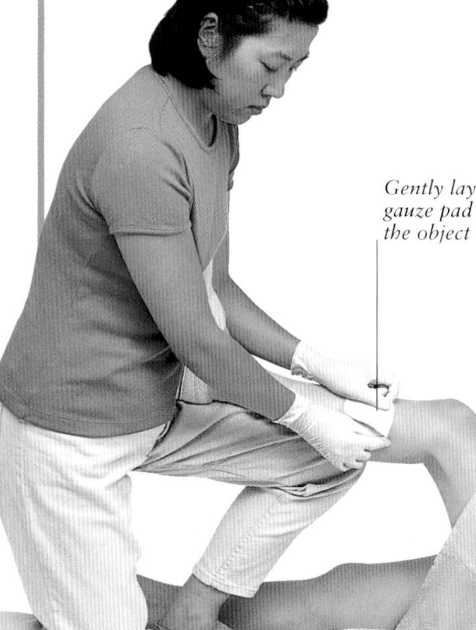

Gently lay gauze pad over the object

Raise the injured part, if possible

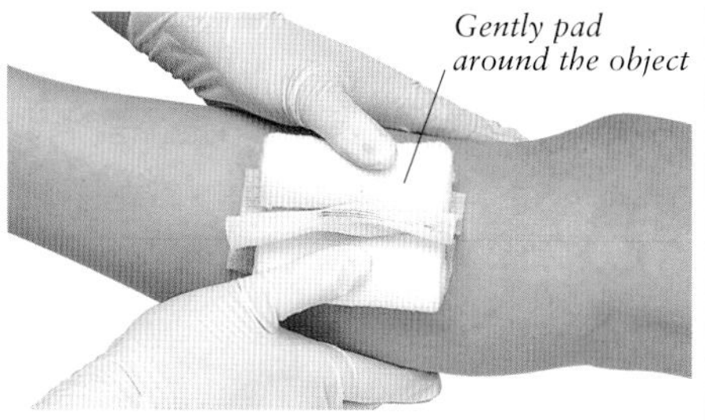

3 Place padding around the protruding object

Very carefully, place padding around either side of the object to protect the wound and to control bleeding.

► **DO NOT** pull the gauze down on the object as you do this.

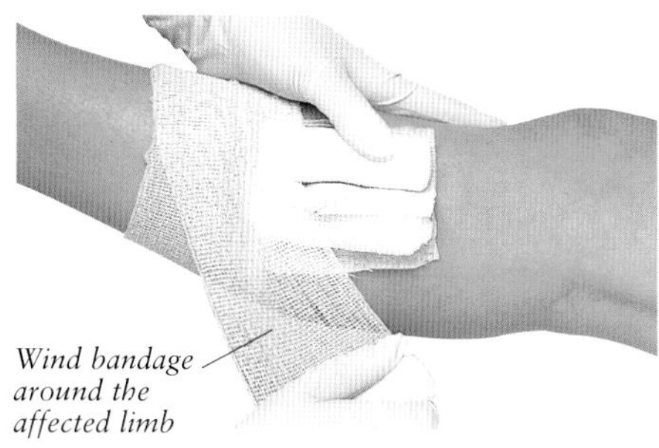

4 Place a bandage over one side of the padding

Place one end of a bandage over the part of the padding nearest to you. Make two straight turns around the casualty's limb.

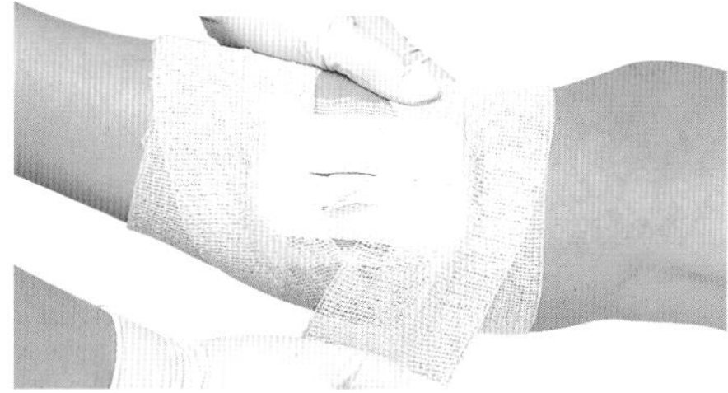

5 Bandage around the limb on either side of padding

Pass the bandage under the limb and wrap it around the other side of the padding.

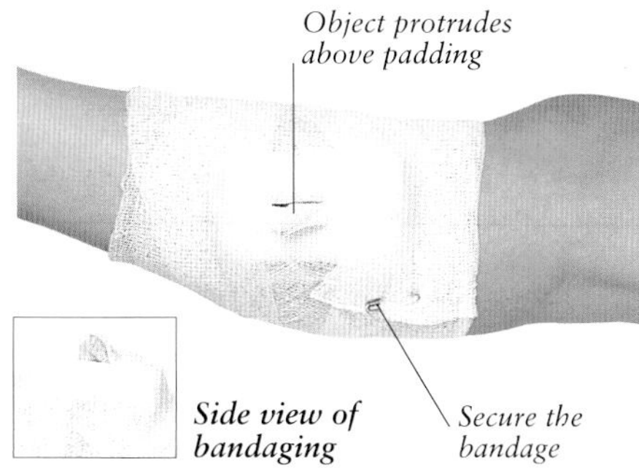

6 Continue diagonal turns above and below the injury

Continue these turns around the limb on either side of the padding until the dressing is firm. Secure the bandage.

IF the object is not protruding at all or is not very high, you can pad around it and bandage directly over it without pressing down on the object (see right).

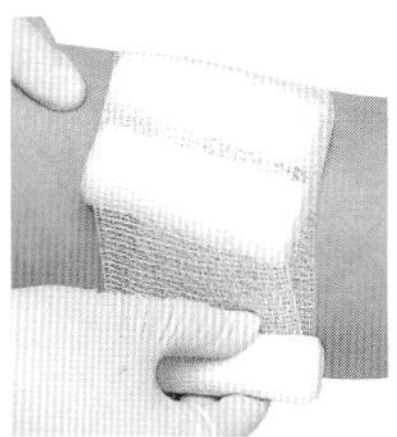

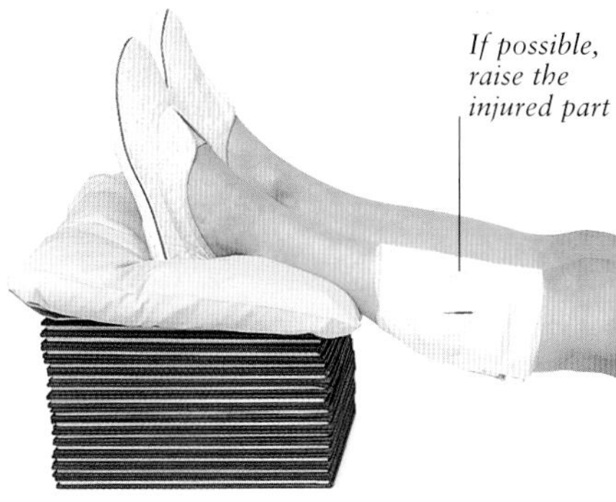

7 Keep the injured limb raised and steady

Keep the injured part raised where possible and as still as you can.

> **!** IF the object is large, in the lower limb, or near a vital organ or an eye,
> **✚ CALL AN AMBULANCE**

BLEEDING FROM THE SCALP

The scalp, the skin that covers the head, may bleed profusely when damaged, making an injury appear more serious than it is. However, a casualty with a head injury must see a doctor because a blow to the head can also cause concussion or fracture the skull (see p. 40).

Aim
- To control bleeding.
- To get the casualty to hospital.

You will need
- Disposable gloves
- Sterile dressings

see *Sterile dressings* p. 32

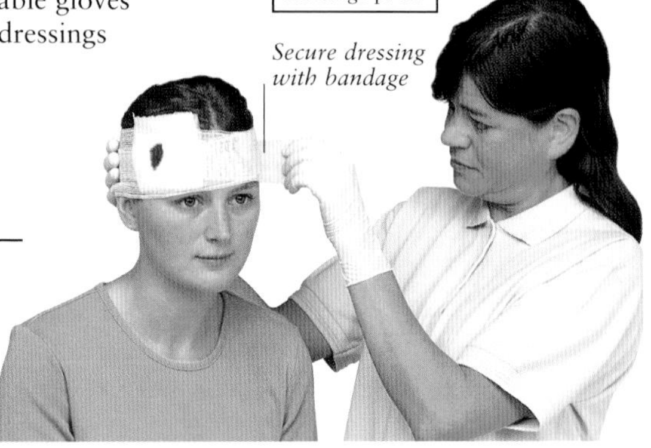

Secure dressing with bandage

1 Cover the wound with a sterile dressing

Gently place a sterile dressing over the wound. Apply direct pressure to the pad and press the sides of the wound together to control bleeding. Secure the sterile dressing with a bandage.

Put dressings on top if blood shows through

2 Apply further dressings if blood shows through

If bleeding shows, secure another sterile dressing on top of the original one.

3 Support casualty in half-sitting position

Help the casualty to lie down with her head and shoulders slightly raised.

☐ TAKE OR SEND THE CASUALTY TO HOSPITAL

! **IF** the casualty becomes unconscious, open the casualty's airway, check the breathing and place the casualty in the recovery position. Be prepared to resuscitate the casualty if necessary (see pp. 16–25).

✚ CALL AN AMBULANCE

Continue to monitor the casualty's breathing, circulation and responses at regular intervals until the emergency services arrive.

see *Recovery position* p. 18

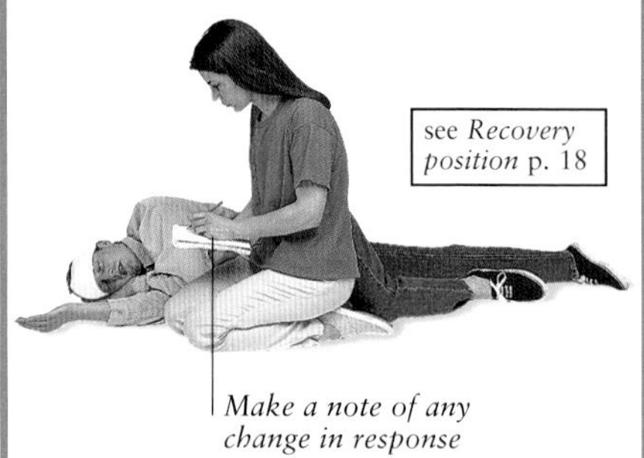

Make a note of any change in response

FROM THE PALM OF THE HAND

This type of injury will bleed a great deal and it can be difficult to apply enough pressure to control it. If nothing is embedded in the wound, treat the injury as shown below. If an object is embedded, treat as described on page 52.

Aim

- To control bleeding.
- To get the casualty to hospital.

You will need

- Disposable gloves
- Sterile dressing
- Triangular bandage

1 Apply direct pressure to the wound

Check the wound to make sure nothing is embedded in it. Apply direct pressure; either you or the casualty can do this.

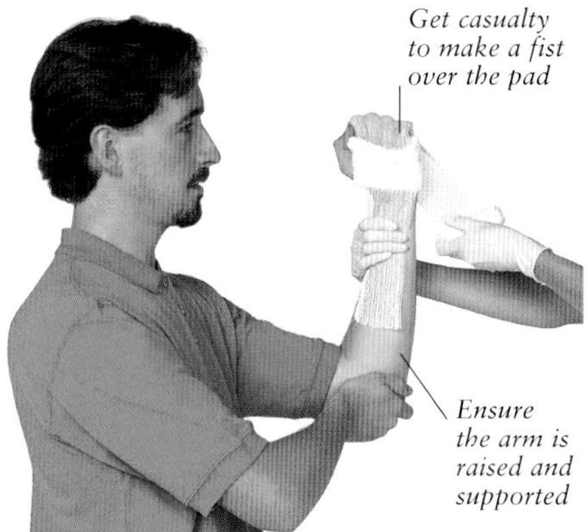

Get casualty to make a fist over the pad

Ensure the arm is raised and supported

2 Raise the casualty's injured hand above chest level

Raise the hand above chest level. Put a sterile dressing on the wound and ask the casualty to clench his fist over the pad.

3 Secure the dressing

With the fist still clenched, secure the dressing with the attached or a separate bandage. Tie a reef knot over the fingers (see p. 35).

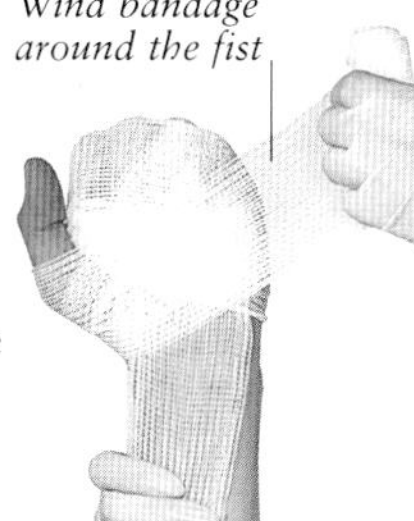

Wind bandage around the fist

4 Check the circulation

Check circulation in the wrist and at the thumb on the injured arm (see p. 34).

IF circulation is reduced, loosen the bandage until it is restored to normal.

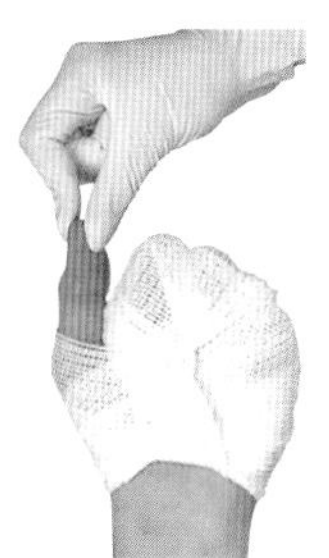

see *Elevation sling* p. 37

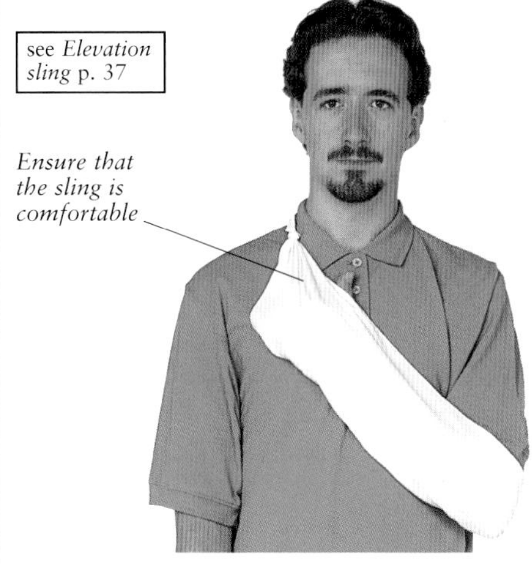

Ensure that the sling is comfortable

5 Place the casualty's arm in an elevation sling

Support the casualty's arm in an elevation sling. Re-check the circulation in the casualty's arm (see p. 34).

☐ TAKE OR SEND THE CASUALTY TO HOSPITAL

BLEEDING FROM THE MOUTH

Cuts to the tongue and lips are usually caused by the casualty's own teeth. Bleeding from the mouth or a tooth socket may also occur immediately after accidental loss of a tooth or some considerable time after a tooth has been removed by a dentist.

Aim

- To keep the airway clear to prevent the casualty choking on blood.
- To control the bleeding.

You will need

- Disposable gloves
- Gauze pad

1 Lean the casualty's head to the injured side

Sit the casualty down and incline her head forwards and towards the injured side.

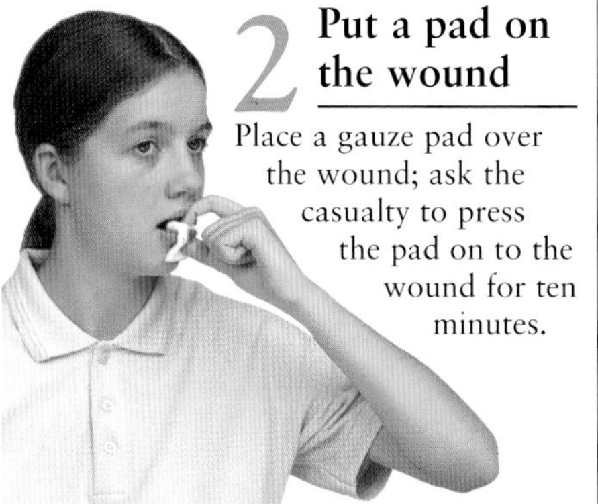

2 Put a pad on the wound

Place a gauze pad over the wound; ask the casualty to press the pad on to the wound for ten minutes.

IMPORTANT

Seek medical or dental advice if the mouth bleeds for longer than 30 minutes and replace soiled gauze pads with fresh ones.

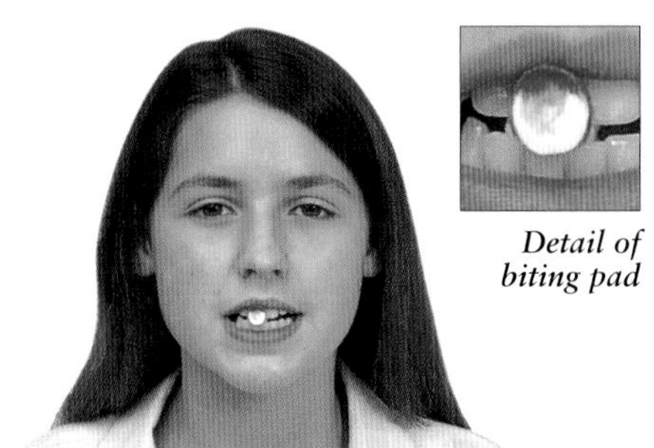

Detail of biting pad

IF the casualty is bleeding from a tooth socket, put a gauze pad over the tooth socket. The pad should be thick enough to stop her top and bottom teeth meeting. Tell her to bite on this for 10–20 minutes.

3 Tell the casualty to avoid hot drinks

Tell the casualty not to drink anything hot for 12 hours after the bleeding has stopped.

Replacing a knocked out tooth

If an adult's tooth has been accidentally knocked out you should replace it in its socket, if possible, with a pad between the top and bottom teeth to keep it in position. Make sure that it is the right way round. Alternatively, the casualty may place it in her cheek or you can keep the tooth in milk or water. The casualty should then be taken or sent to a dentist.

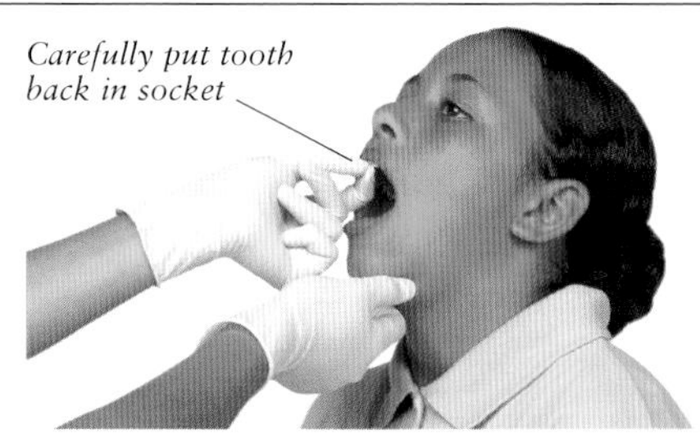

Carefully put tooth back in socket

From the nose

A nosebleed occurs when the delicate blood vessels break either spontaneously or following a blow.

Aim

- To control the bleeding.
- To prevent the casualty from choking.

1 Ask the casualty to sit down and to lean forwards

Sit the casualty down and ask her to lean forwards. Loosen any tight clothing.

2 Pinch the nose

Tell her to pinch her nose in the middle for ten minutes and to breathe through her mouth.

IF bleeding continues, reapply pressure.

3 Advise the casualty to spit out any blood

While she is applying pressure, ask her to spit out any blood in her mouth.

4 Tell the casualty not to blow her nose

Advise the casualty to avoid blowing her nose for several hours after the nosebleed.

IF bleeding has not stopped after half an hour of continuous pressure,

✚ CALL AN AMBULANCE

From the ear

A ruptured eardrum, caused by a foreign body or blow to the head, is the usual cause of a bleeding ear.

Aim

- To allow blood to drain away.
- To minimise the risk of infection.
- To arrange transport to hospital.

You will need

- Disposable gloves
- Sterile dressing

▶ **DO NOT** attempt to plug the ear.

1 Get the casualty to lie down with her head raised

Help the casualty to lie down with her head and shoulders raised. Tilt her head towards the injured side.

see *Sterile dressings* p. 32

2 Gently place a dressing over the injured ear

Place a sterile dressing over the ear and lightly secure it in place.

✚ CALL AN AMBULANCE

IF the casualty becomes unconscious, put her in the recovery position, injured side down to allow fluid to drain out and monitor her condition until help arrives.

IF yellowish bloodstained fluid is coming from either the ear or nose after a blow to the head, this may mean that the casualty has a fractured skull. Cover the ear and lie her down with head and shoulders raised.

✚ CALL AN AMBULANCE

Monitor the casualty carefully.

Cuts and grazes

With small cuts and grazes, the bleeding soon stops of its own accord. However, any break in the skin, even a small one, can allow germs (bacteria) to enter the body. Germs are micro-organisms that are carried by flies or by unwashed hands; if they are allowed to settle on an open wound, they can grow and cause infection. The aim of first aid treatment for this type of injury, therefore, is to clean and dress the wound as soon as possible to prevent an infection developing.

Aim

- To stop the wound from becoming infected.
- To control any bleeding.

You will need

- Disposable gloves
- Sterile gauze swabs or antiseptic wipes
- Plaster or dressing

▶ **DO NOT** handle the open graze or cut with your fingers while you are treating the casualty.

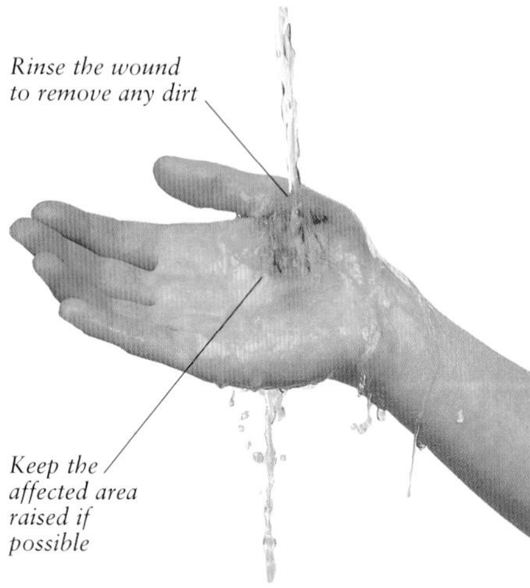

1 Rinse the wound under cold running water

Sit the casualty down. Raise the injured part. Rinse the wound under cold running water to remove any dirt from the wound.

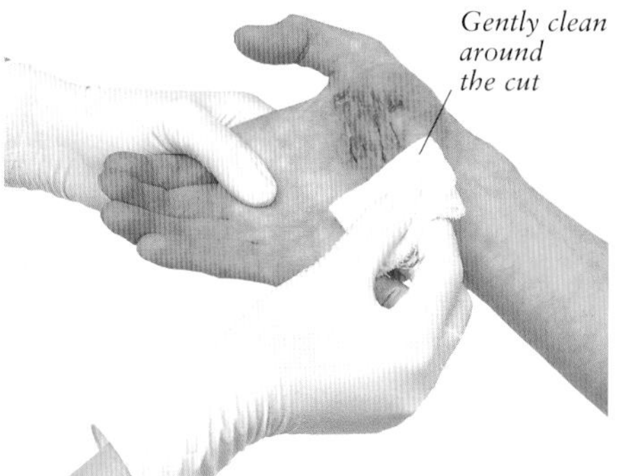

2 Carefully clean the area around the wound

Using sterile gauze swabs, gently clean around the wound. Always work from the wound outwards and use a fresh gauze swab for each stroke.

3 Remove any loose foreign matter from the wound

Carefully remove any loose foreign matter from or around the wound such as glass, metal or gravel.

▶ **DO NOT** try to remove anything that is embedded in the wound; treat as described on page 52.

4 Gently dry the area around the wound

Gently dry the area around the wound with a gauze swab. Be careful not to disturb the wound when you are drying around it.

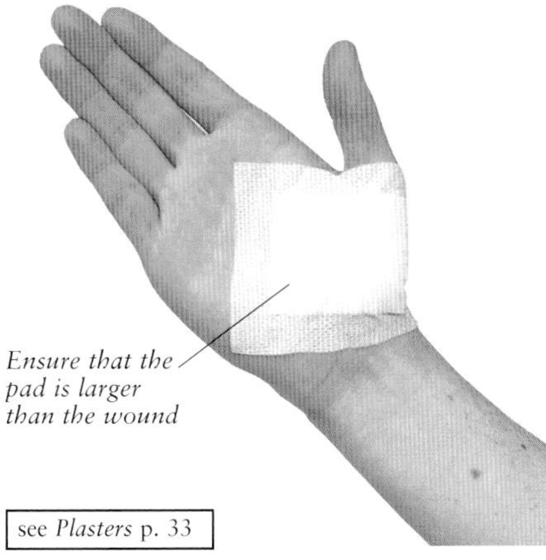
Ensure that the pad is larger than the wound

see *Plasters* p. 33

5 Apply a plaster to the affected area

For a small cut or graze, apply a plaster to the affected area; take care not to touch the sterile part of the plaster.

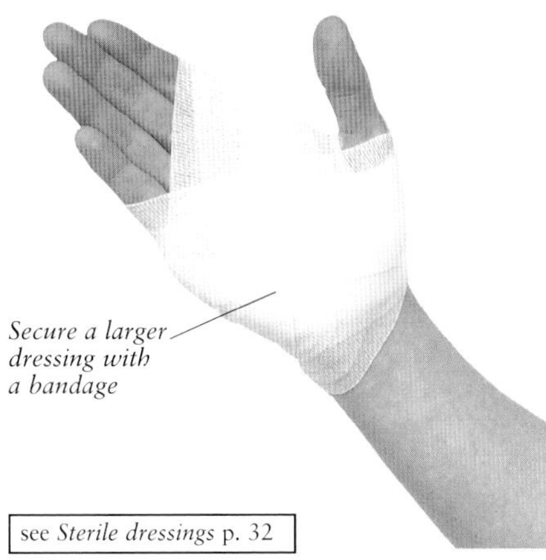
Secure a larger dressing with a bandage

see *Sterile dressings* p. 32

IF the cut or graze is larger, apply a sterile dressing to the affected area and secure it in place with a bandage.

6 Rest the injured part

Rest the injured part and, if possible, keep it in a raised position.

► DO NOT use cotton wool on or near an open wound because this may stick to the wound.

BRUISING

This follows an injury and is bleeding just under the skin or deeper in the tissues. The area often becomes blue-black quite quickly, or the bruise may take a few days to appear.

Aim
- To minimise swelling by cooling the area.

You will need
- Cold compress

see *Cold compresses* p. 33

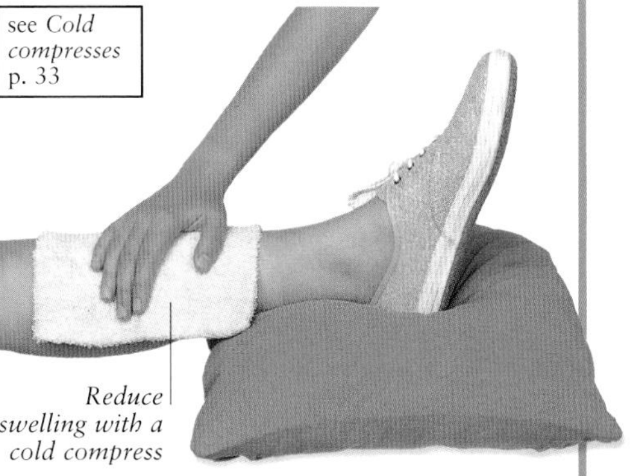
Reduce swelling with a cold compress

1 Apply a cold compress to the bruised area

Place a cold compress on the injury to minimise the swelling.

2 Support the injured area

Support the injured part in the most comfortable position for the casualty; apply a sling if appropriate.

IMPORTANT

A "black eye" is a bruise normally caused by a blow to the face. As it may also cause damage to the eye or skull, you should always make sure that this type of injury is checked by a doctor.

BURNS AND SCALDS

The skin has a number of different layers and has many functions, one of which is to protect the body from invasion by germs. A burn or scald can break this protective barrier, allowing germs to enter the body and cause infection. Serious burns can also cause fluid loss and lead to shock (see p. 51).

WHAT CAUSES BURNS

Burns are caused by extremes of dry heat, such as fires and hot metal, or by extreme cold (cold burns). Scalds cause identical injuries and result from extremes of moist heat such as boiling water or steam. Other burns include chemical burns, caused by strong acids or alkalis; friction burns; radiation burns, caused by exposure to sunlight or radiation and electrical burns caused by direct contact with electricity.

HOW TO RECOGNISE BURNS AND SCALDS

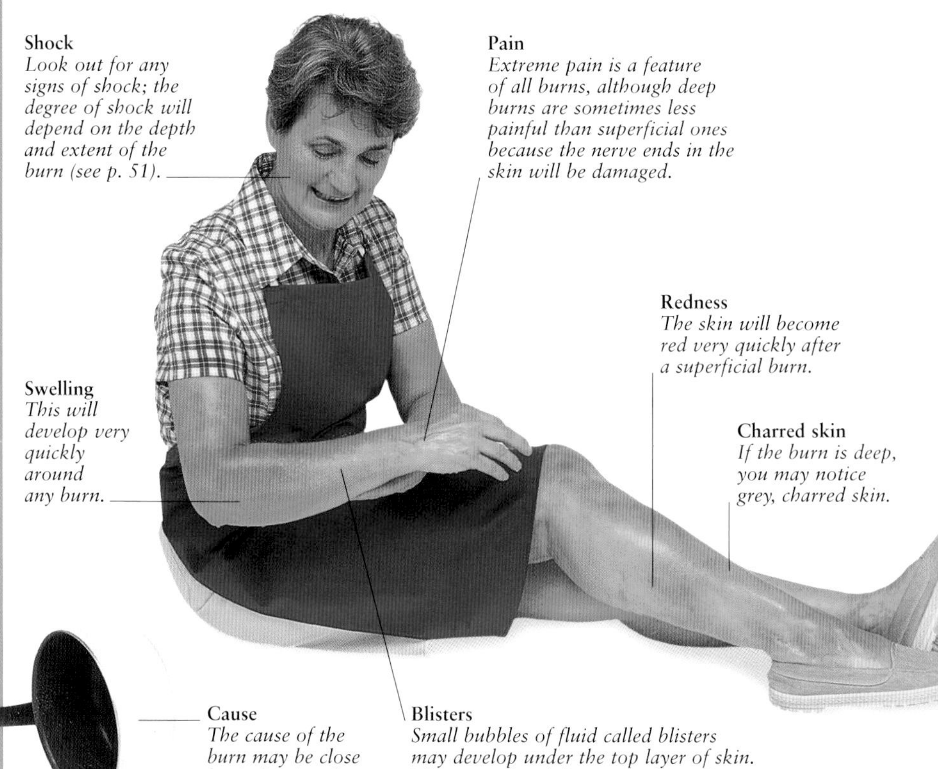

Shock
Look out for any signs of shock; the degree of shock will depend on the depth and extent of the burn (see p. 51).

Pain
Extreme pain is a feature of all burns, although deep burns are sometimes less painful than superficial ones because the nerve ends in the skin will be damaged.

Redness
The skin will become red very quickly after a superficial burn.

Swelling
This will develop very quickly around any burn.

Charred skin
If the burn is deep, you may notice grey, charred skin.

Cause
The cause of the burn may be close by, indicating the type of injury.

Blisters
Small bubbles of fluid called blisters may develop under the top layer of skin. These may break leaving peeling skin and a small red patch of weeping fluid.

HOW BURNS AFFECT YOU

The main risk of a burn is the possibility of infection (see opposite). Burns also cause fluid to weep from the body tissues. The loss of body fluid depletes the fluid part of the blood, called plasma, and if a large enough area of skin is burned, even superficially, shock can develop (see p. 51).

When shock may develop

If more than one tenth of the body surface is burned (an area roughly the size of the surface area of the chest), you can expect a casualty to develop shock. If more than one third of the body is burned, the casualty's life is in danger and urgent hospital treatment is required.

▶ **DO NOT** put any fats, ointments or lotions on a burnt area because these may cause further tissue damage.

▶ **DO NOT** place fluffy materials, such as cotton wool, on burns.

▶ **DO NOT** deliberately break blisters.

▶ **DO NOT** use adhesive dressings or tape to cover a burn.

BEFORE YOU TREAT A BURN

- **Look out for danger**
  Check for any hazards. If you are in danger, do not approach a casualty.

- **Follow the ABC** see *Resuscitation* pp. 16–25
  If the casualty appears unconscious check his responses; if unconscious, open the airway and check breathing; if breathing, put the casualty into the recovery position. Check the circulation and keep the casualty's airway open. Be ready to resuscitate the casualty if necessary.

HOW TO TREAT A BURN

1 Cool the burn

Stop the burning by cooling the affected area as quickly as possible under cold running water to prevent any further tissue damage, reduce swelling, minimise shock and alleviate pain.

2 Check for and treat other injuries

Gently cover area with a sterile dressing or kitchen film to stop infection (see p. 32). Treat other injuries.

3 Treat for shock

Watch for signs of shock and, if necessary, treat the casualty for shock (see p. 51).

4 Get medical help

Assess the seriousness of the casualty's burn; unless the burn is a very small one you should seek further medical aid for the casualty (see p. 62).

> **!** **IF** the burn is near the mouth or throat, is extensive or deep,
> ✚ CALL AN AMBULANCE

TYPES OF BURN

The severity of a burn depends on the type of burn and on the size of the area that is affected. There are three types of burn: superficial, partial-thickness and full-thickness (see below). A casualty with a deep burn may lose the sensation of pain due to nerve and tissue damage.

How burns affect the skin

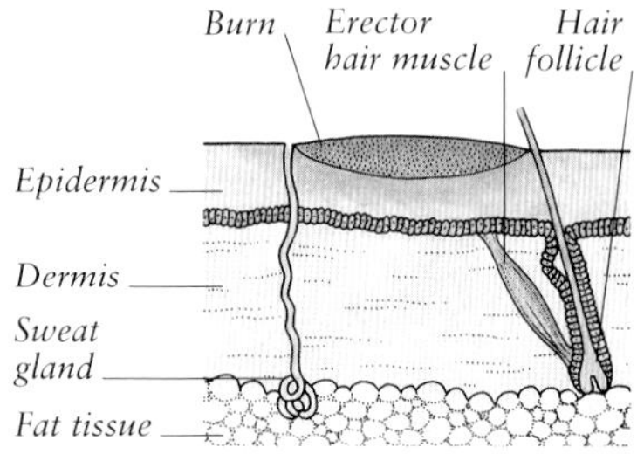

Superficial burn
This affects the top layer of skin only and causes redness and swelling, but is not serious unless extensive. With prompt first aid this should heal within a few days.

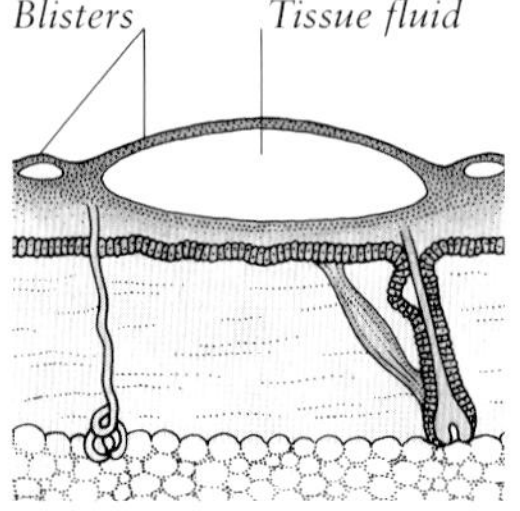

Partial-thickness burn
This deeper burn affects several skin layers, results in blisters and needs medical attention. This type of burn usually heals, but if extensive can be serious and even fatal.

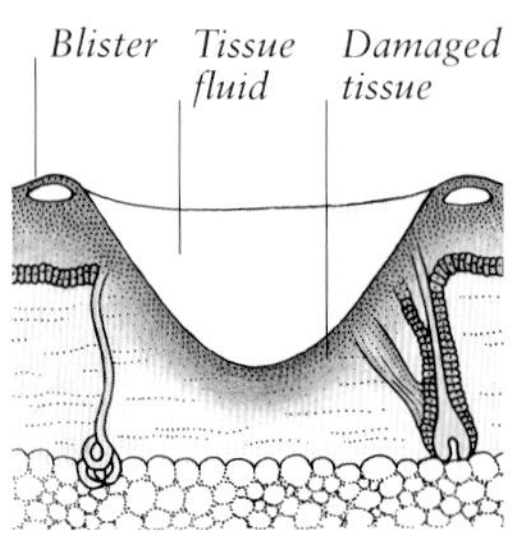

Full-thickness burn
This type of burn affects all the layers of the skin and may also affect the nerves and tissues. The skin may appear pale or charred. This requires urgent medical attention.

CLOTHING ON FIRE

If clothing is on fire, remember this procedure: Stop, Drop, if possible Wrap and Roll (see right). Use a heavy material such as a woollen blanket to wrap around the casualty; do not use anything flammable.

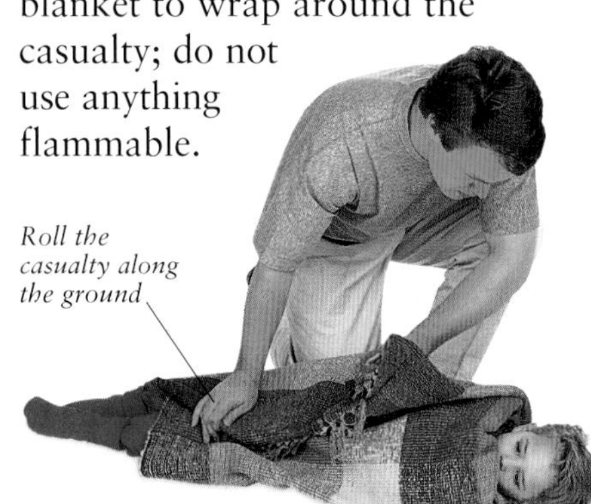

Roll the casualty along the ground

STOP

Stop the casualty moving as movement will fan the flames. Tell him to keep still.

DROP

Make the casualty drop to the floor to stop him burning his neck, face and airway.

WRAP

If possible, wrap the casualty in a coat or blanket to help smother the flames.

ROLL

Roll him on the ground to put out the fire.

Make sure that the casualty's airway is open and treat him for burns and shock.

TREATING SEVERE BURNS

Your aim in treating a deep or extensive burn is to reduce the effect of the heat on the skin and, as far as possible, to prevent germs getting into the burnt area. If a large part of the casualty's body surface is burnt, lay her down, protecting any burnt area from direct contact with the ground, and treat her for shock (see p. 51). If the casualty has been involved in a fire, the airway may also be affected and you should check the casualty's breathing regularly. A severe burn requires urgent hospital treatment to minimise subsequent damage.

Aim

- To relieve the burning and pain.
- To check the casualty's breathing.
- To reduce the risk of infection.
- To get the casualty to hospital.

You will need

- Disposable gloves
- Sterile dressing
- Cold, running water

1 Check for danger

Before you approach and treat the casualty, check for any danger to yourself or to the casualty.

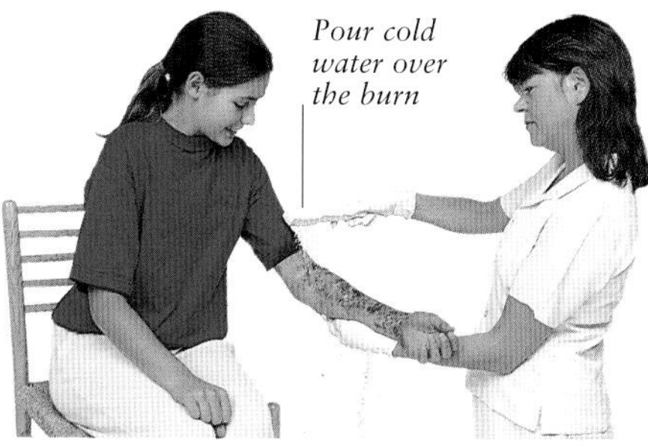

Pour cold water over the burn

2 Cool the burn with running water

Sit or lie the casualty down. Pour cold water over the burn for at least ten minutes; do not let this delay her getting to hospital.

▶ **DO NOT** overcool a serious burn because this could cause hypothermia.

✚ CALL AN AMBULANCE

3 Check the casualty's breathing

While cooling the burn and waiting for the ambulance, constantly check the casualty's breathing. Be ready to resuscitate if necessary (see pp. 16–25).

IF possible, remove any restricting clothes or jewellery from the affected limb while the limb is in water but do not remove anything that is sticking to the skin.

4 Cover the injury

When the pain is relieved, cover the burnt area with a sterile dressing (see p. 32).

IF no dressing is available, cover the burn with a clean polythene bag or kitchen film.

5 If necessary, treat for shock

Sit or lie the casualty down and, if necessary, treat for shock (see p. 51). Constantly reassure the casualty.

6 Monitor the casualty's condition

Monitor the breathing, pulse and responses until help arrives. If necessary, be ready to resuscitate (see pp. 16–25).

FACE AND HEAD BURNS

Burns to the mouth or throat are dangerous because they can cause rapid swelling and inflammation of the airway. If the burn is in the mouth or throat, external signs of burning may be evident such as soot around the mouth. There is no first-aid treatment for an extreme case; the swelling will rapidly block the airway and immediate medical aid is required. Burns to the face and head may also affect the casualty's airway depending on the severity of the burn (see box, below).

BURNS TO THE AIRWAY

SIGNS AND SYMPTOMS

- If severe, the casualty will develop features of shock (see p. 51).
- The casualty's mouth, throat and head may be very painful.
- Difficulty in breathing.
- Damaged skin around the mouth.

! **IF** unconscious, open the airway, check breathing and place in the recovery position. Be prepared to resuscitate (see pp. 16–25).

see *Recovery position* p. 18

Aim

- To get the casualty to hospital immediately.
- To keep the airway open.

1 Get urgent medical assistance

✚ CALL AN AMBULANCE

Tell the control officer that you suspect burns to the airway so that the correct treatment can be ready.

2 Loosen tight clothing

Take any steps possible to improve the casualty's air supply; for example, loosen tight clothing around the neck. Give oxygen if you are trained to do so.

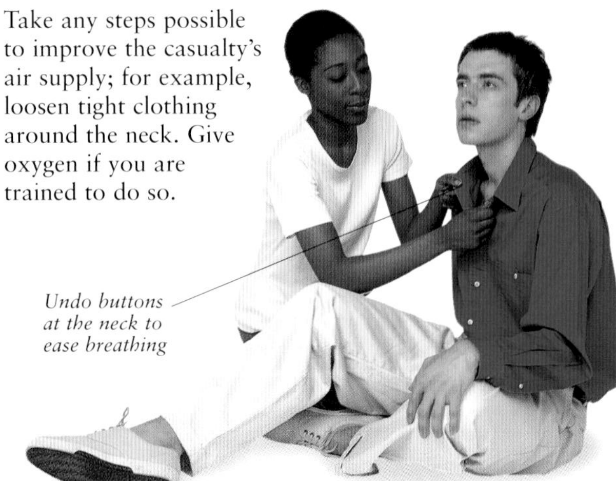

Undo buttons at the neck to ease breathing

Burns to the head

One of the main concerns of a head burn is swelling near the airway (see above). Keep the burnt area cool; if possible, use a watering can or something similar to pour water gently over the head. If the burn is near the throat, nose or mouth, call an ambulance immediately and be ready to resuscitate (see pp. 16–25). Do not put tight dressings on the burn; if necessary, hold a dressing on until help arrives.

Chemical burns

Many substances used in the home, in the workshop or by industry can seriously damage the skin or eyes; you must act quickly to wash the chemical off the casualty's skin or out of the eyes. Protect yourself and ensure that any contaminated water can drain away freely.

SIGNS AND SYMPTOMS

- Chemicals near the casualty.
- Stinging pain.
- Discolouration, swelling and blistering.

Chemical burns to the eye:

- Casualty may be unable to open eye.
- Swelling around eye and watering.

BURNS TO THE SKIN

Aim

- To wash the chemical away.

You will need

- Disposable gloves
- Sterile dressing
- Cold running water

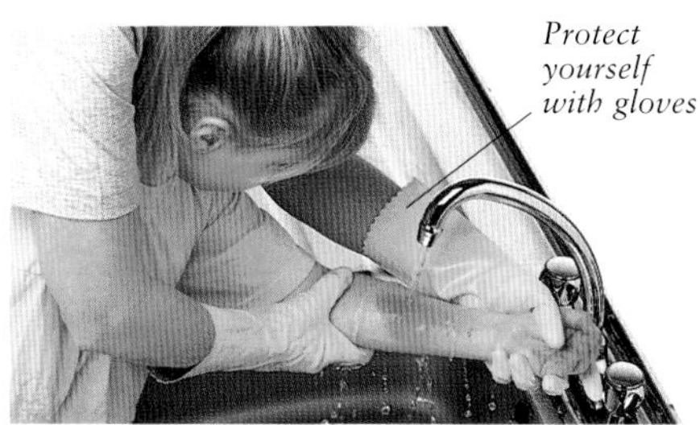

Protect yourself with gloves

1 Flood the affected area with water

Flood the area by holding the injured part under cold running water for at least 20 minutes to disperse the chemical.

2 Remove contaminated clothing

Take any contaminated clothing off the casualty while you are flooding the area. After washing the area, cover the burn with a sterile dressing and, if necessary, treat the casualty for shock (see p. 51).

☐ TAKE OR SEND THE CASUALTY TO HOSPITAL

BURNS TO THE EYE

Aim

- To wash the chemical away.

You will need

- Disposable gloves
- Sterile dressing
- Cold running water

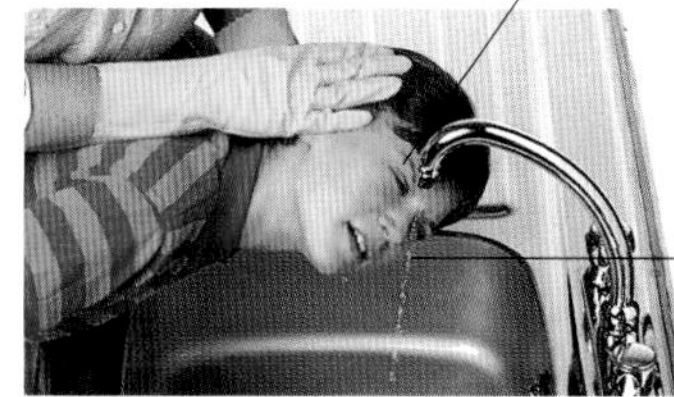

Position eye under the tap

Ensure water drains away from the face

1 Pour cold water into the affected eye

Hold the affected side of the face under cold running water for at least 20 minutes. Position the head so that contaminated water does not run down the face.

☐ TAKE OR SEND THE CASUALTY TO HOSPITAL

2 Cover the affected eye with a pad

Once the pain has eased, ask the casualty to hold a sterile pad lightly over the eye.

IF the casualty is still in pain, continue pouring water over the eye.

ELECTRICAL BURNS

Burns can occur when an electrical current passes through the body, and may be visible at the point where electricity enters or leaves the body. An electrical burn may cause internal damage and lead to unconsciousness. If consciousness is lost, open the airway, check breathing and be prepared to resuscitate (see pp. 16–25). Electrical burns at home are low-voltage and it is safe to switch the current off; do not approach a person who has suffered high-voltage burns (see below and p. 6).

SIGNS AND SYMPTOMS

- ▶ Casualty may be unconscious.
- ▶ Swollen, charred skin.
- ▶ Shock may develop.
- ▶ A high-voltage burn may leave a brownish residue on the skin.

Aim

- To treat visible burns and any shock.
- To get the casualty to hospital.

You will need

- Cold running water
- Sterile dressing or non-fluffy material

1 Break the contact with the electrical source

Where possible, turn off the electricity or break contact with the source (see p. 6).

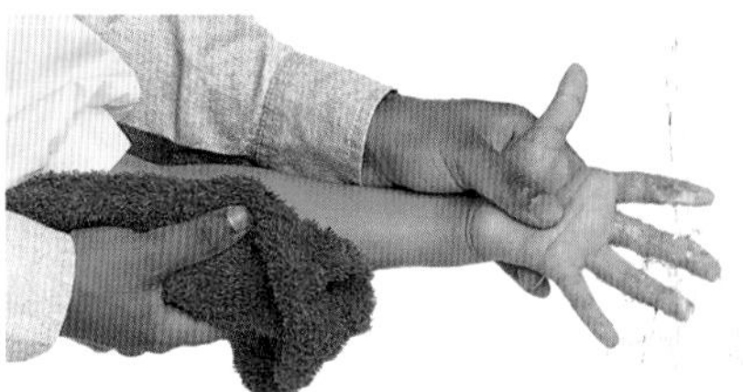

2 Pour cold water over the affected area to cool it

Pour cold water over the burn to cool the area and cut away any clothing from around the burn.

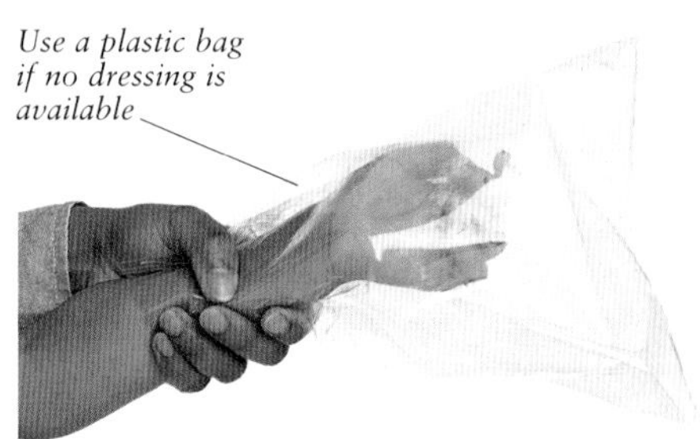

Use a plastic bag if no dressing is available

3 Protect the affected area from infection

Protect the affected area from infection by placing a sterile dressing over it. Alternatively, if you have no dressing, place some clean non-fluffy material, such as kitchen film, over the affected area or put a clean plastic bag over a burnt hand or foot and secure it with some tape.

✚ CALL AN AMBULANCE

4 Reassure the casualty

Reassure the casualty and, if necessary, treat for shock (see p. 51).

! **IF** a casualty has suffered a high-voltage burn, do not approach him until the current has been officially switched off and you are given permission to approach the casualty. Keep yourself and bystanders at a safe distance of 18 m (20 yd).

FRICTION BURNS

Friction burns occur when skin is rubbed against a surface. Blisters develop when tissue fluid leaks from the damaged area and collects under the outer layer of the skin.

Aim

- To relieve pain.
- To minimise the risk of infection.

You will need

- Soap and cold clean water
- Clean pad
- Plaster or sterile dressing, or some clean, non-fluffy material

1 Clean the affected area

Wash the area carefully with soap and water and rinse with clean water.

2 Gently dry the affected area

Dry the area and the surrounding skin very thoroughly, using a gentle patting action, with a clean pad.

3 Apply a plaster

Carefully cover the blister with a plaster (see p. 33). Make sure that the pad of the plaster is larger than the blister.

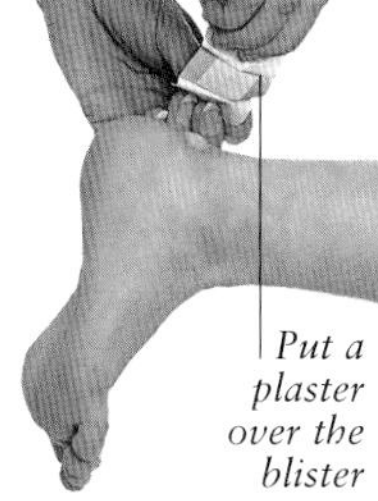

Put a plaster over the blister

IF the blister is very large, use a sterile dressing or piece of non-fluffy material, secured with adhesive tape or a bandage.

IMPORTANT

Never deliberately break a blister.

SUNBURN

Over-exposure to the sun's rays without adequate protection can result in widespread superficial burns and, in severe cases, blistering. The casualty's skin will become red and feel very hot.

Aim

- To take the casualty out of the sun.
- To relieve discomfort and pain.

You will need

- Cold water and a sponge
- Drinking water
- Calamine lotion/after-sun cream

1 Cover the casualty's skin with light clothing

Cover the skin with light clothing and move the casualty into the shade.

2 Keep the casualty cool

Cool the burnt area by sponging gently with cold water. Give the casualty frequent sips of water.

IF the sunburn is mild, apply calamine or after-sun cream to the skin.

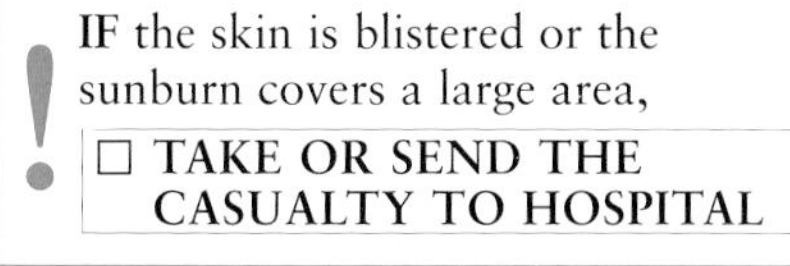

! IF the skin is blistered or the sunburn covers a large area,

☐ TAKE OR SEND THE CASUALTY TO HOSPITAL

IMPORTANT

Prevention is better than cure. Wear sunscreen when in the sun and do not stay in the sun for too long; expose the body slowly to the sun, wear a hat and only uncover small areas of the body at a time.

BONE, JOINT AND MUSCLE

The body is supported by a scaffolding of bones called the *skeleton* (see p. 70). Normally bones are very strong but they can break or crack if struck, twisted or over-stressed; this is called a *break* or *fracture*. Injuries can also occur if the ligaments that support joints are torn or the muscles are torn or strained. It can often be difficult to distinguish between a bone, joint or muscle injury without an X-ray; if in any doubt, treat as a break. For treatment of minor sprains or strains, see page 78.

HOW TO RECOGNISE A BREAK OR SOFT TISSUE INJURY

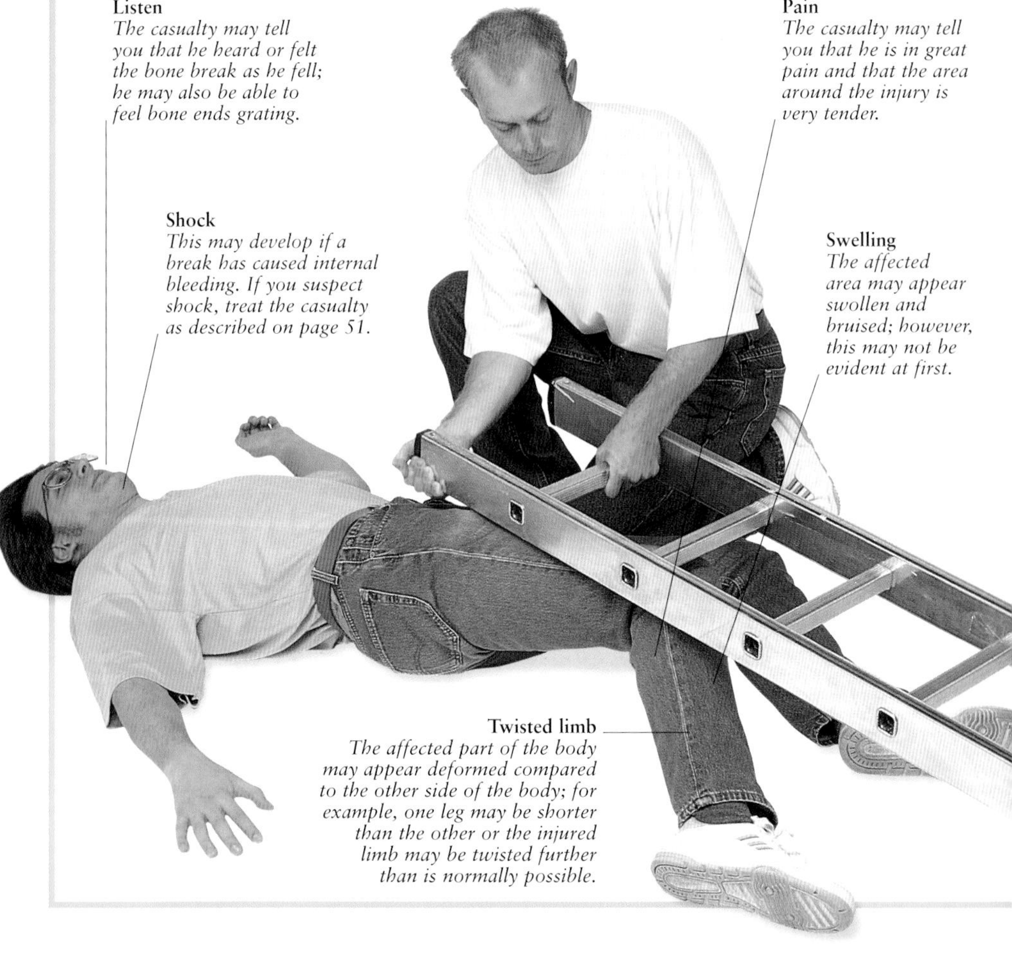

Listen
The casualty may tell you that he heard or felt the bone break as he fell; he may also be able to feel bone ends grating.

Pain
The casualty may tell you that he is in great pain and that the area around the injury is very tender.

Shock
This may develop if a break has caused internal bleeding. If you suspect shock, treat the casualty as described on page 51.

Swelling
The affected area may appear swollen and bruised; however, this may not be evident at first.

Twisted limb
The affected part of the body may appear deformed compared to the other side of the body; for example, one leg may be shorter than the other or the injured limb may be twisted further than is normally possible.

INJURIES

BROKEN BONES

Bones have important blood vessels, nerves and organs that lie alongside them, therefore all breaks must be handled extremely carefully. The aim of first aid is to prevent further damage by avoiding any unnecessary movement.

How breaks occur

A bone may be broken by direct force, in which case the break will be at the point of impact. Alternatively, a broken bone could be caused by indirect force, which means that the break occurs at some distance from the point of impact or is the result of a bad twist.

Casualties with suspected breaks should, as far as possible, be treated in the position in which you find them; steady and support the injured bone with one hand above and the other below the site of the injury. Specific treatment for the most common breaks is described later in this section. There are, however, general rules of treatment that must be followed for all suspected broken bones (see right).

JOINT AND MUSCLE INJURIES

Sprains and dislocations are injuries to the joints between the bones. Strains are injuries to the muscles that move the bones and can be extremely painful. In some instances, particularly a dislocated joint, it can be difficult to distinguish between this type of injury and a break. If in any doubt, treat as a broken bone.

BEFORE TREATING INJURIES

- **Look out for danger**
  Check for any hazards. If in danger, do not approach a casualty.

- **Follow the ABC**
  see *Resuscitation* pp. 16–25
  If casualty appears unconscious check the responses; if unconscious, open the airway and check breathing; if breathing, put in the recovery position. Check the circulation. Keep the airway open. Be ready to resuscitate if necessary.

HOW TO TREAT INJURIES

1 Do not move the casualty, if possible

Do not move the casualty unless he is in danger. In that case, support the injury while others move him.

2 Support and cushion the injured part

Use both hands to support the injury above and below the joints. If possible, put coats or cushions around it.

3 Protect open wounds from infection

Cover any open wound with a sterile dressing or clean non-fluffy material.

IF the injury is in the leg,

✚ CALL AN AMBULANCE

IF the injury is in the upper body,

☐ TAKE OR SEND THE CASUALTY TO HOSPITAL

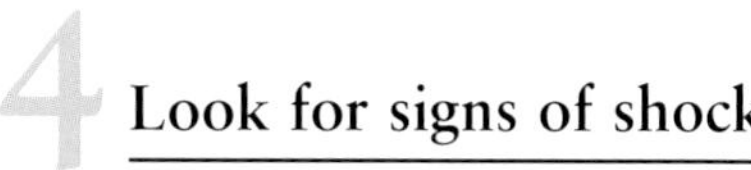

4 Look for signs of shock

If necessary, treat for shock (see p. 51).

THE SKELETON, JOINTS AND MUSCLES

The bones of the skeleton protect and surround vital organs and act as levers for muscle to pull against. Bones meet at joints and muscles help bones to move at joints.

THE SKULL

This consists of a number of bones united to form a dome-like vault with a flat base; the brain is contained within the skull.

THE SPINE

The spinal bones (vertebrae) extend from the base of the skull to the base of the back, enclosing and protecting the spinal cord. Each bone is separated by a disc or "cushion" of cartilage.

THE RIBCAGE

This consists of twelve pairs of bones (ribs) that curve round from the spine to the breastbone to form a cage that contains, among other organs, the heart and lungs.

THE PELVIS

This "basin" consists of two hip bones joined to the bottom of the spine; each has a socket into which the thigh bone fits. It protects the bladder, bowel and blood vessels and nerves that supply lower limbs.

JOINTS AND MUSCLES

The points at which bones meet are joints; these are held together by tough bands of fibre called ligaments. The most important joints are the hinge joints, such as the knee and elbow joints, which allow to-and-fro movement in one plane only, and the ball and socket joints, such as the hip and shoulder joints, which permit pivoting and rotation of the limb. Bones are moved at joints by muscles that contract and pull one bone towards another.

The skeleton

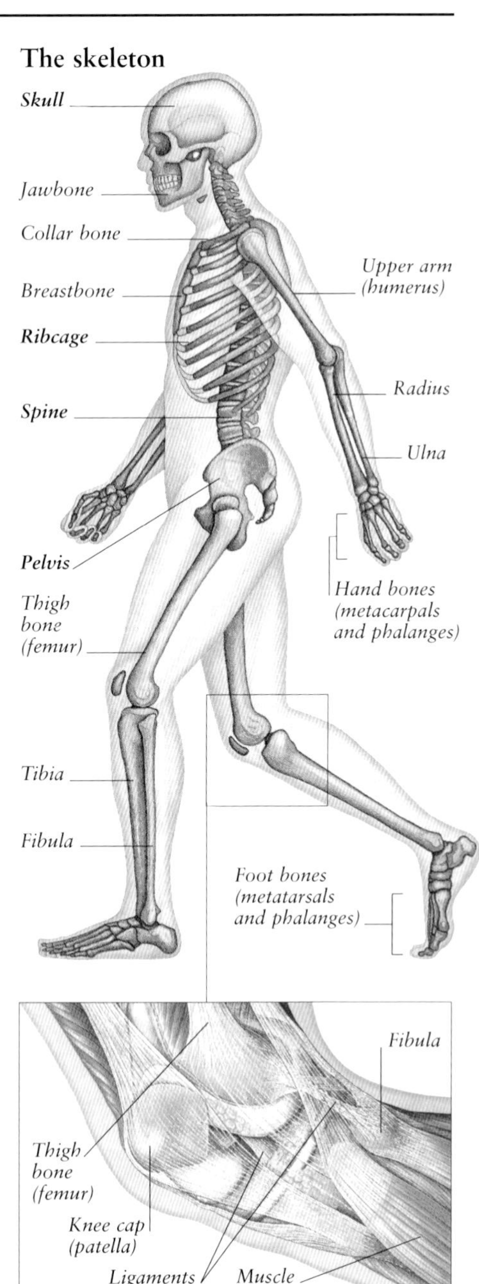

Hinge joint at the knee

Treating broken bones

A casualty with a suspected broken bone must receive hospital treatment. Keep the injured part steady and supported as shown below until help arrives and do not move a casualty with a suspected fracture unless his or her life is in immediate danger.

Types of break

There are many types of break; the two main divisions are open and closed. Both types can be complicated if a broken bone end presses on or damages adjacent nerves, blood vessels or organs.

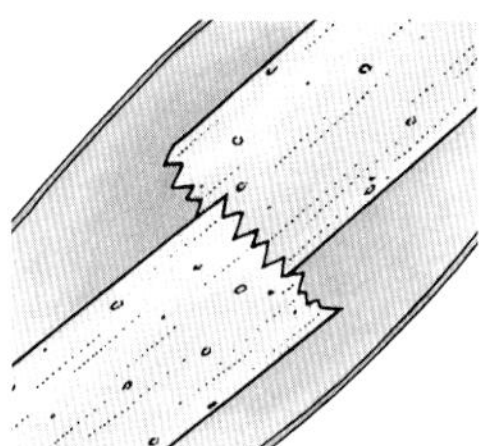

Closed break
This is a break where the skin around the injury is not damaged.

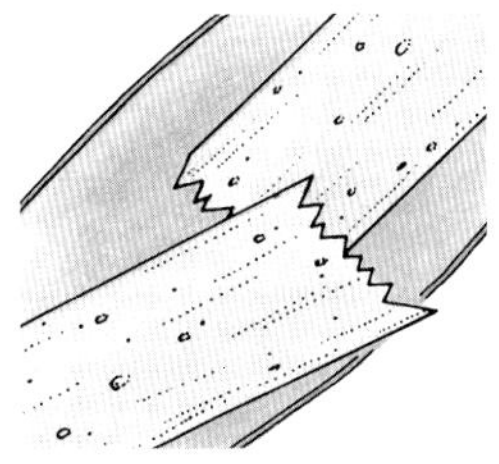

Open break
This occurs when a wound leads to a broken bone that may or may not stick out of the skin.

Aim

- To keep the injured limb steady.
- To get the casualty to hospital.

1 Steady and support the injured part

Advise the casualty to keep still and make him as comfortable as possible. Steady and support the injured part placing your hands above and below the point of injury.

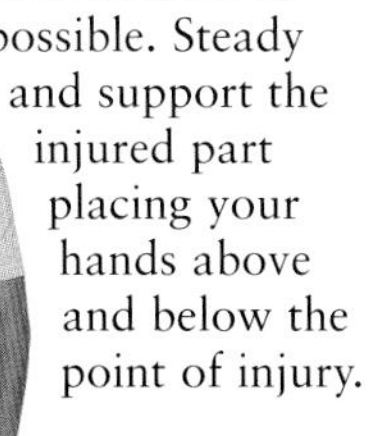

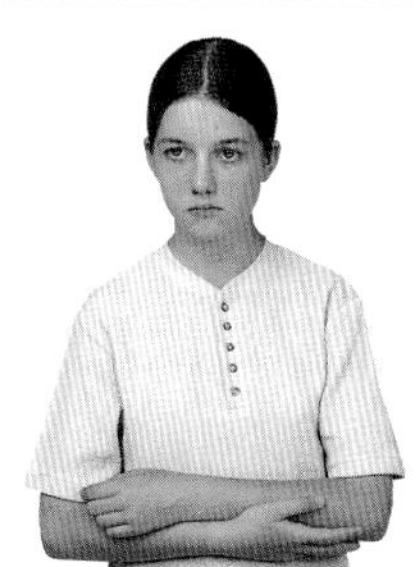

IF the casualty has a broken arm, place it across her chest and get her to support it with her uninjured arm.

✚ CALL AN AMBULANCE

2 If necessary, treat the casualty for shock

If the casualty shows signs of shock (see p. 51), treat him accordingly, but do not raise his limb if this causes pain.

► **DO NOT** allow the casualty to eat or drink anything as he may need a general anaesthetic.

Open breaks

Treat open breaks carefully to stop germs entering the bone and causing serious infection. Support the injury (see above) and loosely cover the wound with a sterile dressing. Arrange for the casualty to be taken to hospital.

BROKEN JAW

This is usually the result of a direct blow to the jaw. A blow to one side of the jaw can also fracture the other side.

SIGNS AND SYMPTOMS

- Pain when speaking, chewing or swallowing; casualty may dribble.
- Bloodstained saliva.
- Displaced teeth in the mouth.
- Swelling and/or unevenness along one side of the jaw.

Aim

- To keep the airway open.
- To get the casualty to hospital.

You will need

- Padding

1 Lean the head forwards and remove displaced teeth

Lean the casualty forwards to keep the airway open and to let fluid drain. Remove displaced teeth or loose dentures. Give the teeth to the doctor or ambulance crew.

2 Hold a pad over the jaw

Get the casualty to loosely hold a soft pad over the injured area. Support his head and jaw if he feels sick.

> ! IF the casualty is seriously injured or unconscious, put him in the recovery position (see p. 18) with the injured side down and a pad under his head.
>
> ✚ CALL AN AMBULANCE

BROKEN CHEEK OR NOSE

A fracture of the cheekbone or nose can cause uncomfortable swelling and may block the casualty's airway.

SIGNS AND SYMPTOMS

- Swelling.
- Pain around the affected area.

Aim

- To reduce swelling.
- To get the casualty to hospital.

You will need

- Cold compress

see *Cold compresses*, p. 33

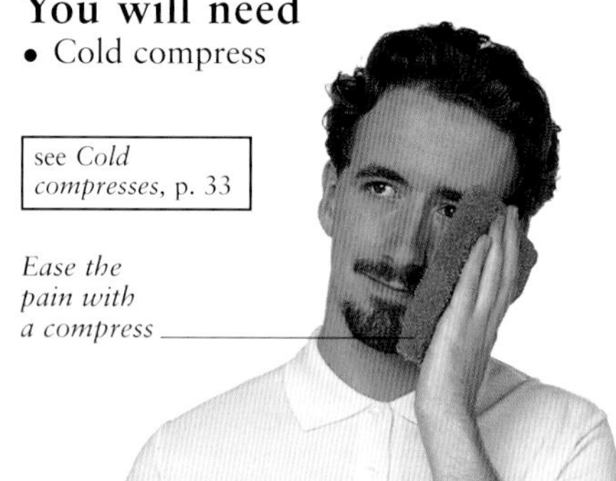

Ease the pain with a compress

1 Put a cold compress on the injured area

Place a cold compress or pad on the injured area to reduce swelling and pain.

2 Treat for a nosebleed, if necessary

If necessary, treat the casualty for a nosebleed (see p. 57).

☐ TAKE OR SEND THE CASUALTY TO HOSPITAL

IF clear-yellowish fluid is leaking from the nose, assume the casualty has a skull fracture and treat appropriately (see p. 40).

BROKEN COLLAR BONE

A broken collar bone is most commonly caused by indirect force, for example, from a fall onto an outstretched hand. This transmits force along the casualty's forearm and upper arm to the collar bone.

SIGNS AND SYMPTOMS

- Casualty may be supporting her arm on the injured side.
- Casualty may incline her head towards the injury to relieve the pain.
- Casualty may be reluctant to move the arm on her injured side.
- Swelling or deformity may be visible at the site of injury.

Aim

- To immobilise the injured part.
- To get the casualty to hospital.

You will need

- Padding
- 2 triangular bandages

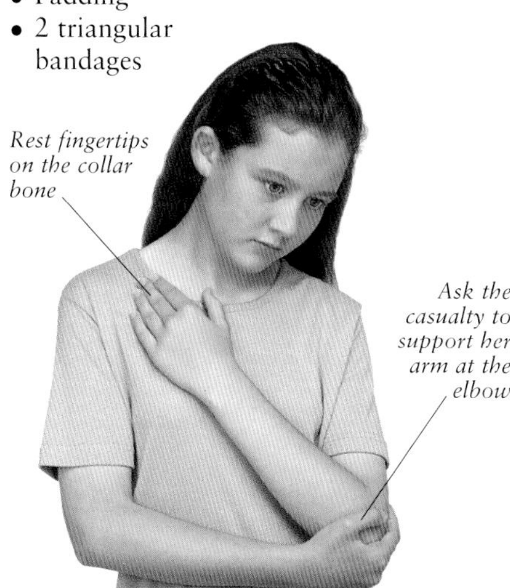

Rest fingertips on the collar bone

Ask the casualty to support her arm at the elbow

1 Position the arm ready to apply an elevation sling

Help the casualty to position her arm on the injured side so that her fingertips are almost resting on the opposite shoulder.

2 Support the arm in an elevation sling

Support the casualty's arm in an elevation sling. Try to move the arm as little as possible when applying the sling.

3 Place soft padding between the arm and the chest

Make the casualty more comfortable by placing soft padding, for example a folded towel, between her upper arm and chest.

see *Elevation sling* p. 37

see *Broad-fold bandage* p. 31

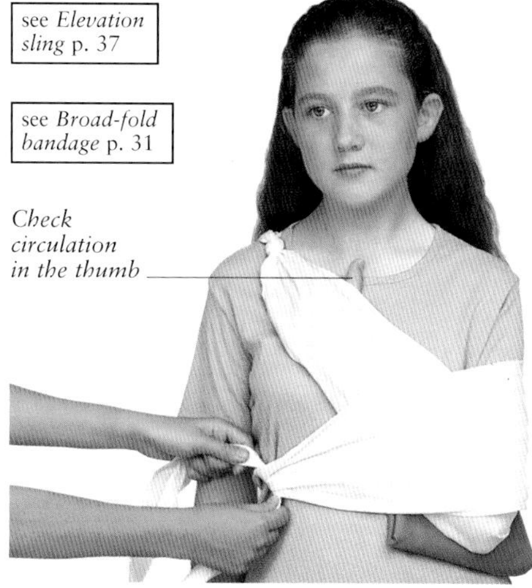

Check circulation in the thumb

4 Secure the injured arm to the casualty's chest

Secure the injured limb to the casualty's chest by applying a broad-fold bandage over the sling and around her body. Check circulation in the thumb (see p. 34).

☐ TAKE OR SEND THE CASUALTY TO HOSPITAL

BROKEN ARM

A break can occur anywhere along the upper arm or forearm bones and may involve an elbow or wrist joint. Never forcibly bend an arm.

SIGNS AND SYMPTOMS

- Pain and tenderness.
- Inability to use the injured arm.
- Deformity, swelling, possible bruising.

Aim

- To immobilise the injured part.
- To get the casualty to hospital.

You will need

- Padding
- 2 triangular bandages

1 Gently bend the casualty's arm at the elbow

If possible, bend the casualty's arm at the elbow so that her arm is across her trunk. Pad between the fracture site and the body.

! **IF** the casualty can't bend her arm, lay her down; pad around the elbow.
✚ CALL AN AMBULANCE

2 Support the casualty's arm in an arm sling

Put the arm in a sling. For extra support, secure the casualty's arm to her body with a broad-fold bandage ensuring you avoid the site of the break.

see *Arm sling* p. 36

see *Broad-fold bandage* p. 31

☐ TAKE OR SEND THE CASUALTY TO HOSPITAL

BROKEN HAND AND FINGERS

Breaks in the bones of the hands or fingers are often caused by crushing and the break may be open with some bleeding.

SIGNS AND SYMPTOMS

- Pain and tenderness.
- Inability to use the injured hand.
- Deformity, swelling, possible bleeding.

Aim

- To immobilise and raise the injured part.
- To get the casualty to hospital.

You will need

- Disposable gloves
- Sterile dressing
- Padding
- 2 triangular bandages

1 Raise the injured hand

Raise the hand to control bleeding and swelling. If possible, remove jewellery.

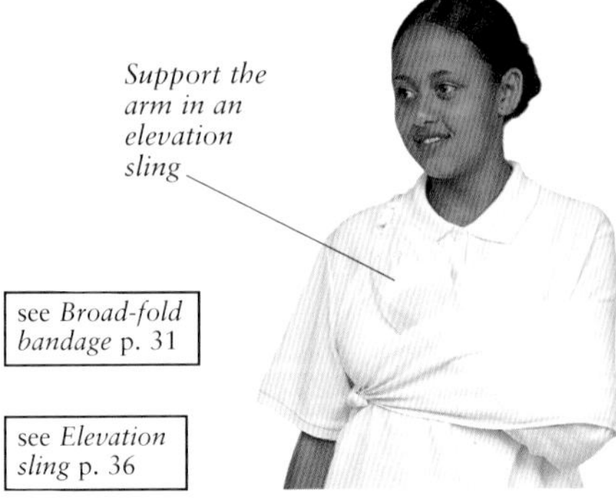

Support the arm in an elevation sling

see *Broad-fold bandage* p. 31

see *Elevation sling* p. 36

2 Put the casualty's arm in an elevation sling

If bleeding, put a dressing on (see p. 32) and pad around the hand. Apply a sling; secure this with a broad-fold bandage.

☐ TAKE OR SEND THE CASUALTY TO HOSPITAL

Broken ribs

Broken ribs are splinted naturally because they are attached to the ribcage. To treat a broken rib, support the arm on the affected side to relieve the pain.

SIGNS AND SYMPTOMS

- Some swelling.
- Casualty may feel a sharp pain in his side, worsened by taking deep breaths, coughing or movement.
- Tenderness around the affected ribs.
- There may be a crackling sound.

Aim

- To support the casualty's chest.
- To get the casualty to hospital.

You will need

- Triangular bandage

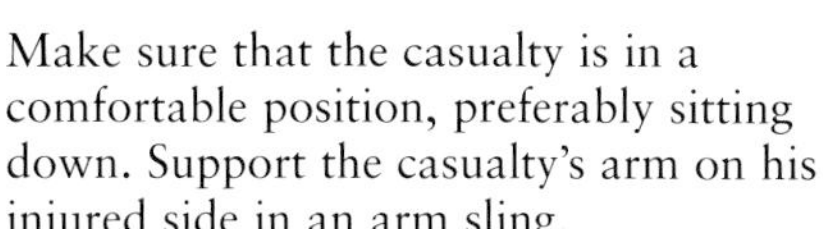

Support the arm in a sling

see *Arm sling* p. 36

Make sure that the casualty is in a comfortable position, preferably sitting down. Support the casualty's arm on his injured side in an arm sling.

☐ TAKE OR SEND THE CASUALTY TO HOSPITAL

! **IF** a chest injury damages several ribs, breathing may be badly affected. Lean the casualty on his injured side in a half-sitting position.

✚ CALL AN AMBULANCE

Broken pelvis

A fractured pelvis must be handled with great care because there may be internal injuries.

SIGNS AND SYMPTOMS

- Pain, swelling, loss of movement.
- Casualty may wish to pass urine, which may be bloodstained.
- Possible internal bleeding (see p. 51).

Aim

- To get the casualty to hospital.

You will need

- Cushion/rolled-up coat

1 Place soft padding under the casualty's knees

Help the casualty onto his back with his legs straight or knees slightly bent. Put a cushion or rolled-up coat under his knees.

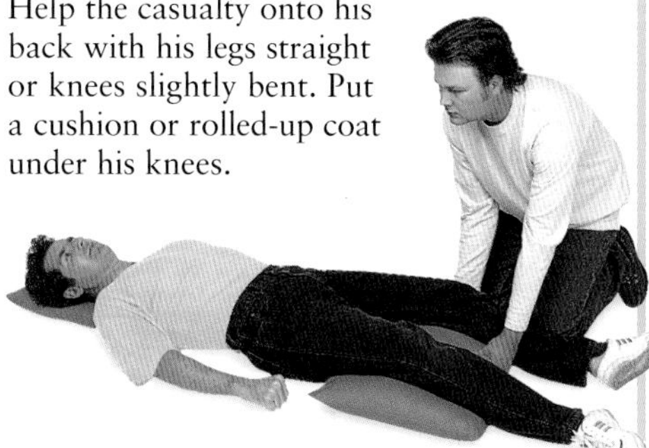

2 Treat for shock, if necessary

Treat the casualty for shock (see p. 51); reassure him and keep him warm. Do not allow the casualty to eat or drink.

✚ CALL AN AMBULANCE

3 Monitor the casualty until help arrives

Monitor the casualty's breathing, circulation and responses continually until the ambulance arrives.

BACK INJURIES

Injuries to the back may be serious because they may affect the spinal cord, which contains the nerves that control many of the body's functions. Damage to the spinal cord can result in paralysis of the body below the injured area. You should suspect a spinal injury if the casualty has fallen awkwardly, especially from a height, and particularly if the casualty has a head injury, or is experiencing any loss of feeling or movement. Mild back injuries can also be made worse by incorrect handling.

SIGNS AND SYMPTOMS

The casualty may tell you that he:

- is tender around his back.
- can feel shooting pains or "electric shocks" in his limbs and/or his trunk.
- is unable to feel or move his legs if the injury is in the lower back or unable to move any limb at all if the injury is at his neck level.

Aim

- To prevent further injury.
- To get the casualty to hospital.

You will need

- Coats/towels
- Blanket

► **DO NOT** move the casualty unless his life is in danger.

1 Align the casualty's head, neck and spine

Advise the casualty not to move. Place your hands over his ears to support the head in a neutral position with the head, neck and spine aligned.

2 Support the head and neck

Use rolled-up coats or towels to protect and splint the head, neck and shoulders. Cover the casualty with a blanket.

✚ CALL AN AMBULANCE

Overhead view showing alignment of the body

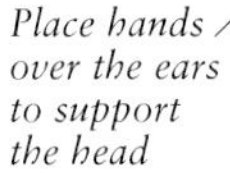

Place hands over the ears to support the head

Put padding around the head

IF the casualty is unconscious, place him in a modified recovery position to protect his airway: roll him on his side with his head and trunk aligned at all times.

Broken leg

A broken leg is a serious injury; the thigh bone has a rich blood supply and a break can cause severe internal bleeding. The shin bone is just below the skin and a break may be open (see p. 71).

SIGNS AND SYMPTOMS

- Pain, swelling, loss of movement.
- Shock may develop.
- There may be an open wound.
- The injured leg may appear shortened.
- The foot, and possibly the knee, may be turned sideways.

Aim

- To support the injured leg.
- To get the casualty to hospital.

Keep the limb steady

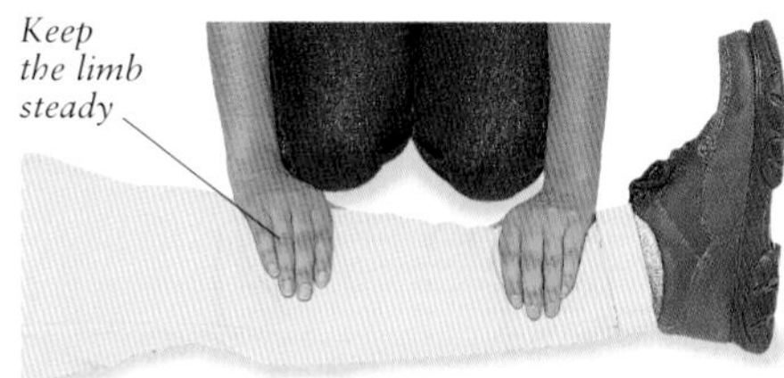

1 Support the injured leg on either side of the break

Carefully help the casualty to lie down and gently steady and support the casualty's leg with your hands at the joints above and below the site of the break.

2 Treat any wounds

Cover any open breaks with a sterile dressing (see p. 32).

✚ CALL AN AMBULANCE

Support the injured leg until help arrives. If necessary, treat for shock (see p. 51).

Knee injuries

It can be difficult to tell whether a person has a broken knee-cap or has damaged a cartilage or ligament. If in doubt, treat as described below. The knee-cap can be broken by a direct blow or split by a violent pull from the thigh muscles attached to it.

SIGNS AND SYMPTOMS

- General features of a broken bone will be present (see p. 68).

Aim

- To prevent further injury.
- To get the casualty to hospital.

You will need

- 2–3 small pillows/coats
- Bandages

1 Make the casualty comfortable

Help the casualty to lie on her back and steady her leg in a comfortable position. Place a small pillow under her knee and rolled coats and/or pillows around her leg.

see *Conforming bandages* p. 34

Keep the leg steady and supported

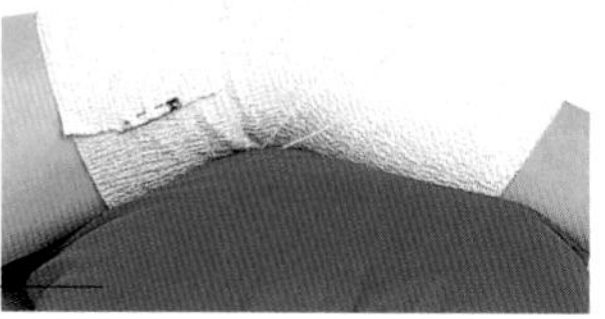

2 Bandage the casualty's injured knee

Bandaging is not essential but the casualty may find it more comfortable. Surround the knee with soft padding; bandage it gently, allowing for swelling.

✚ CALL AN AMBULANCE

SPRAINS AND STRAINS

A sprain occurs when the ligaments that hold the bones together at the joints (see p. 70) are stretched or torn. This is usually very painful and can easily be mistaken for a broken bone (see p. 68). A strain occurs when the muscles and tendons are torn by a sudden movement or violent contraction.

SIGNS AND SYMPTOMS

- Swelling of damaged area.
- Pain and tenderness around the affected area made worse by movement.
- Inability to move a joint; if the injury is at the knee or ankle, the casualty may be unable to stand on the affected limb.
- Gradual bruising of affected area.

Aim

- To reduce swelling and pain.
- To get the casualty to hospital, if necessary, or seek medical aid.

You will need

- Cold compress
- Cotton wool padding and bandage

Follow the RICE procedure if you suspect a sprain or a strain.

R	I	C	E
Rest	*Ice*	*Compress*	*Elevate*

1 Rest and raise the injury

Sit or lay the casualty down and rest the injured part in a comfortable position.

see *Cold compresses* p. 33

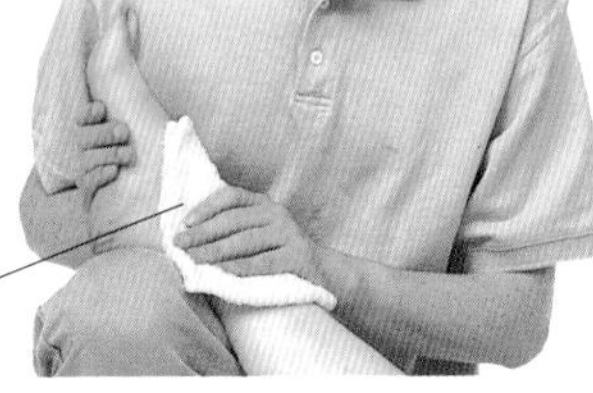

Reduce swelling with a compress

2 Apply a cold compress to the affected limb

Apply an ice pack or cold pad to reduce blood flow and minimise swelling.

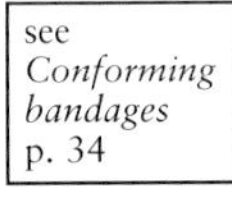

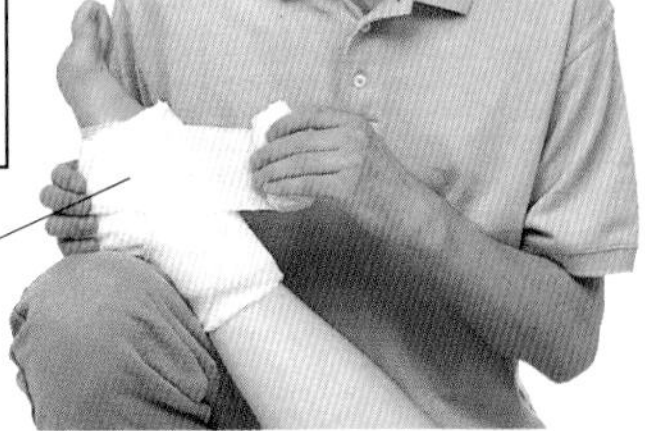

Bandage around the padding

3 Compress the injury with some soft padding

Apply gentle pressure by compressing the injury with soft padding or securing the compress with a bandage.

4 Elevate the injured limb

Raise and support the casualty's injured limb to minimise any bruising. If the injury is to the casualty's wrist, elbow or shoulder, support the affected arm with an arm sling (see p. 36).

IF you suspect a serious injury, for example, the casualty is in great pain and unable to move the affected limb,

☐ TAKE OR SEND THE CASUALTY TO HOSPITAL

for an X-ray diagnosis.

IF the injury appears to be minor,

■ ADVISE THE CASUALTY TO SPEAK TO A DOCTOR

DISLOCATED JOINT

A dislocation is the displacement of bones at a joint. It is normally caused by a particularly violent or awkward twisting strain on the joint, which also tears the ligaments that are supporting it.

SIGNS AND SYMPTOMS

- Casualty may feel a sickening pain around the affected joint.
- Inability to move the affected joint.
- Swelling around the affected area.
- Severe deformity at the site of the injury, particularly visible when compared to the other side of the body.

Aim

- To keep the injured limb supported.
- To get the casualty to hospital.

You will need

- Pillows/blankets
- Triangular bandage

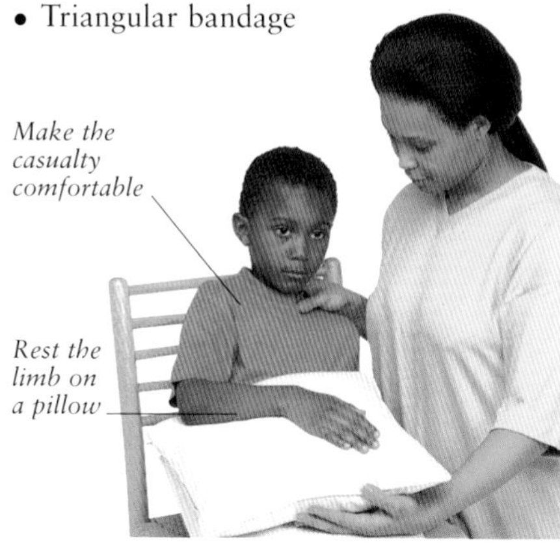

Make the casualty comfortable

Rest the limb on a pillow

Help the casualty into the position he finds most comfortable. Support the injured limb with pillows, rolled blankets and/or an arm sling as applicable.

✚ CALL AN AMBULANCE

CRAMP

This is sudden pain caused by a tightening, or contraction, of one muscle or a group of muscles. Cramp can normally be relieved by stretching the affected muscles.

Aim

- To relieve the pain.

IF a person has been sweating heavily he or she may develop cramp. To relieve this, give him or her a tumbler of water containing a quarter of a teaspoonful of salt (see Heat exhaustion, p. 89).

IN THE HAND

Straighten the casualty's bent fingers by stretching them backwards. You or the casualty can massage the affected hand to further relieve the cramp.

IN THE FOOT

Straighten the casualty's bent toes by pushing them upwards and help her to stand on the ball of her foot.

IN THE CALF

Straighten the knee and pull the foot up to the shin as far as possible. Massage the calf muscles.

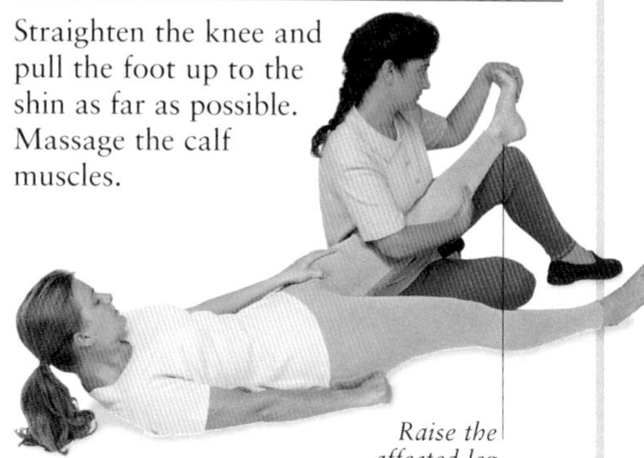

Raise the affected leg

IN THE BACK OF THE THIGH

Straighten the casualty's knee by pulling her leg up and forwards, and gently but firmly press the knee down.

POISONING

Poisons are substances that result in temporary or permanent damage to the body if taken in sufficient quantities. The effects on the casualty vary according to the type of poison and how it has been taken. Try to find out what was taken and how much: ask bystanders and, if the casualty is conscious, ask what happened as soon as possible, in case she loses consciousness.

HOW TO RECOGNISE POISONING

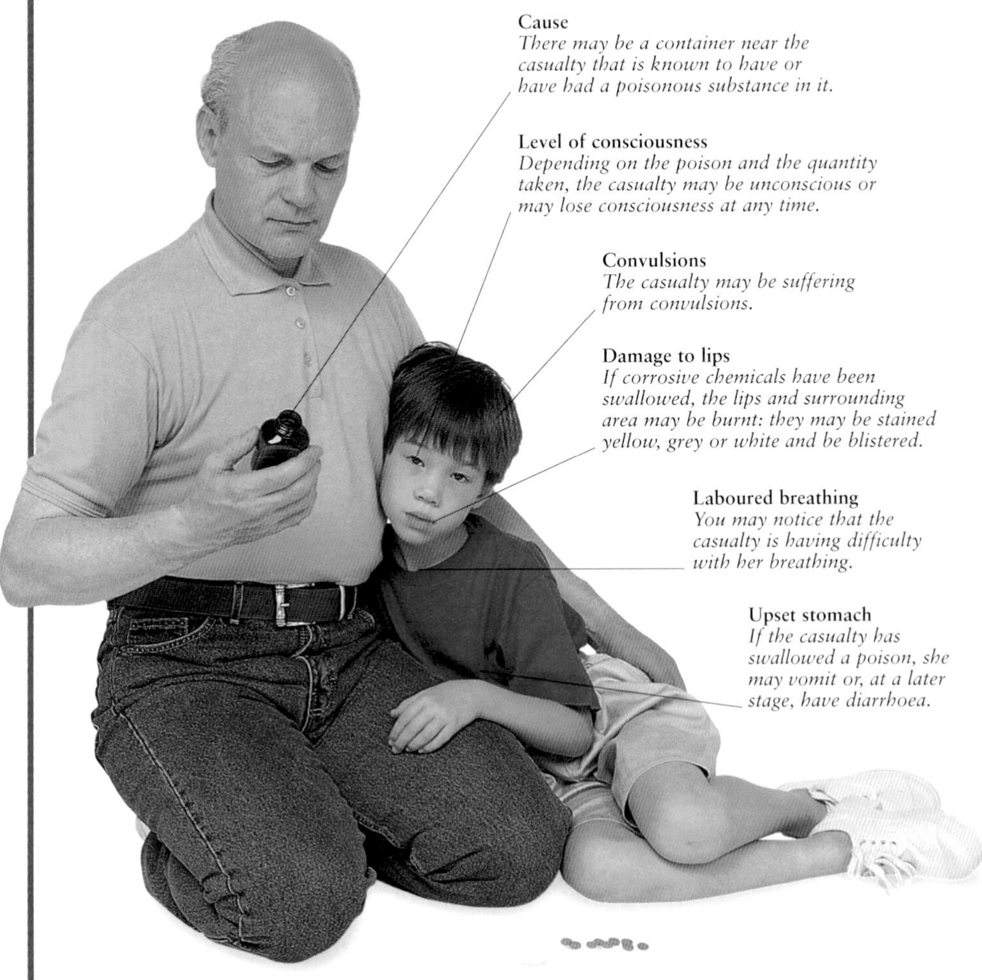

Cause
There may be a container near the casualty that is known to have or have had a poisonous substance in it.

Level of consciousness
Depending on the poison and the quantity taken, the casualty may be unconscious or may lose consciousness at any time.

Convulsions
The casualty may be suffering from convulsions.

Damage to lips
If corrosive chemicals have been swallowed, the lips and surrounding area may be burnt: they may be stained yellow, grey or white and be blistered.

Laboured breathing
You may notice that the casualty is having difficulty with her breathing.

Upset stomach
If the casualty has swallowed a poison, she may vomit or, at a later stage, have diarrhoea.

HOW POISONS ENTER THE BODY

Poisons can enter the body in several different ways:
- by being swallowed;
- by being inhaled;
- by being injected under the skin, for example, by hypodermic syringe, or from animal or insect bites or stings;
- by absorption through the skin, for example, when using agricultural or garden weed killers or insecticides.
- by being splashed into the eye.

IMPORTANT

- **Take care not to get any of the poison on yourself.**
- **If the casualty has swallowed a corrosive poison, never try to force her to vomit because a poisonous substance that has burnt going into the casualty's stomach will burn again coming up.**
- **Do not leave the casualty alone unless you have to in order to call an ambulance.**
- **If you have young children, keep poisonous household substances, for example bleach, out of their reach, not under the kitchen sink. Also, make sure that all tablets or medicines are locked in a cupboard.**

BEFORE YOU TREAT FOR POISONING

- **Look out for danger**
  Check for any hazards. If you are in danger, do not approach a casualty.

- **Follow the ABC**
  see *Resuscitation* pp. 16–25
  If the casualty appears unconscious check the responses. If unconscious, open the airway and check breathing. If breathing, put in the recovery position. Check the circulation and keep the airway open. Be ready to resuscitate if necessary.

HOW TO TREAT FOR POISONING

✚ CALL AN AMBULANCE

1 Give details of the poison, if known

Tell the emergency services what you think the casualty has taken; the person taking the call may be able to tell you what to do while you are waiting for the ambulance to arrive.

2 Give tablets or medicine to the ambulance crew

Give the ambulance crew any tablets and/or medicine or containers that you have found near the casualty or any sample of vomit; they will help the hospital to identify the type of poison.

IF you need to give the casualty artificial ventilation, be careful not to get any of the poison on your own mouth. If possible, wash the poison off the casualty's face before you start artificial ventilation, or use the mouth-to-nose method (see pp. 20–21).

3 Monitor the casualty's responses

If the casualty is conscious, monitor and record her responses regularly to catch any signs of deterioration or loss of consciousness.

IF the casualty has taken a corrosive poison, give her sips of water or milk.

HOW POISONS AFFECT YOU

Poisons can affect many different parts of the body if taken in sufficient quantity and the damage that they cause can be temporary or permanent and sometimes fatal. There are various ways in which poisons can enter the body. They can be swallowed, inhaled, injected, absorbed through the skin or splashed, for example, into the eye.

THE BRAIN

If the brain is affected by a poison, this may cause convulsions, confusion and the casualty may lose consciousness.

THE LUNGS

If a poison is inhaled and reaches the lungs, the casualty may experience serious difficulty in breathing.

THE HEART

Certain harmful drugs can cause an irregular heartbeat and, in severe cases, can lead to cardiac arrest.

THE LIVER AND KIDNEYS

The liver and kidneys act as the body's waste disposal system and usually filter out any harmful substances, for example, alcohol. However, if a large amount of poison enters the body, the liver and kidneys may suffer serious damage.

THE DIGESTIVE SYSTEM

If a poison reaches the digestive system, this can cause severe vomiting, diarrhoea and abdominal pains.

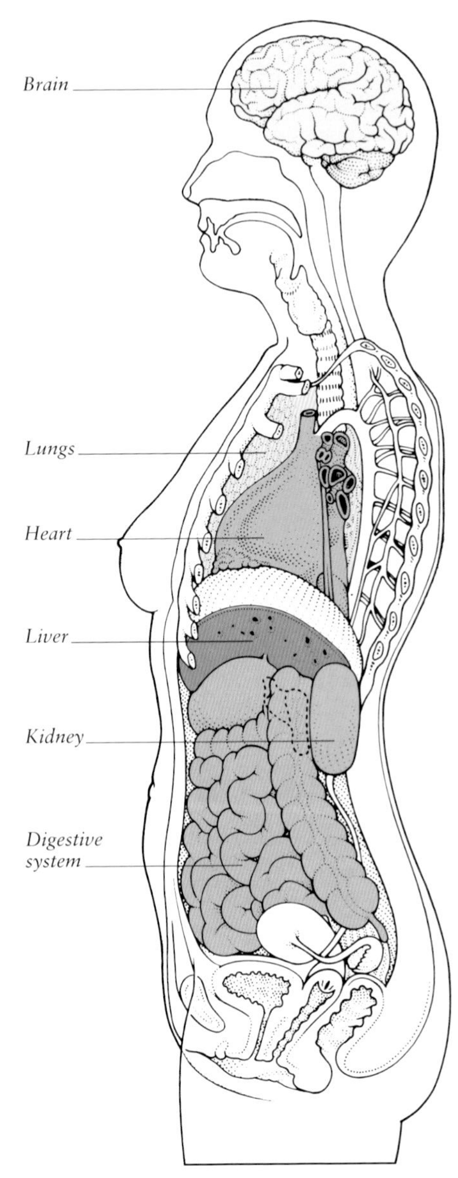

Other effects of poisons

Other areas that may be affected by the ingestion of, or contact with, a poison include external areas, such as the skin or the eyes, which may be splashed with a poison. The lips, mouth and throat may be burnt if the casualty has swallowed a corrosive poison.

ANAPHYLACTIC SHOCK

This is a severe allergic reaction that may occur after an insect bite or after eating certain foods, such as peanuts. The reaction can be fast: the casualty may find it hard to breathe and will need urgent medical aid. Some people are aware that they are susceptible to this condition and carry a dose of adrenaline on them at all times, which is likely to be in the form of a syringe called an Epi-pen. Help the casualty to take the drug or, if you are trained to do so, administer it yourself.

SIGNS AND SYMPTOMS

- Anxiety and difficulty in breathing; the casualty may wheeze.
- Blotchy, red skin.
- Puffy eyes.
- Pulse becomes fast.
- Face and neck may become swollen.

Remain calm and reassure the casualty

Make the casualty as comfortable as possible

Aim

- To get the casualty to hospital immediately.

✚ CALL AN AMBULANCE

Give the crew any information that will help to identify the cause of the attack. Help the casualty into a sitting position to ease any breathing difficulties. Help him with any medication, such as an Epi-pen.

! IF the casualty becomes unconscious at any stage during the anaphylactic reaction, open the airway and check the breathing. Place him in the recovery position and, if necessary, be prepared to resuscitate him (see pp. 16–25).

see *Recovery position* p. 18

Bites and stings

Most bites and stings cause little more than temporary discomfort. There are some people, however, who are particularly sensitive to the poison or venom injected by snake or insect bites, and they may suffer from a severe reaction called anaphylactic shock (see p. 83). If a casualty experiences this reaction, he or she will require urgent hospital treatment.

Insect stings

Insects, such as bees, leave a small sting embedded in the skin that should be removed. Wasp and hornet stings are more alarming than dangerous.

Aim

- To remove the sting.
- To relieve pain and swelling.

Grasp sting as close to skin as possible

You will need

- A pair of tweezers
- Cold compress

1 Carefully remove a visible sting

If the sting is still in the skin, remove it with a pair of tweezers. Hold them close to the skin and pull the sting out. Avoid squeezing the sac at the top of the sting because it will force more poison into the casualty.

2 Apply a cold compress

Apply a cold compress to reduce pain and swelling.

Place a compress over the area

see *Cold compresses* p. 33

3 Rest the injured part

Rest the injured part until pain and swelling subside.

IF pain and swelling persist, ☎ CALL A DOCTOR

! **IF** the casualty shows any signs of anaphylactic shock (see p. 83),
✚ CALL AN AMBULANCE

Stings to the mouth

A sting inside the mouth or throat can be very serious, as the swelling it causes can obstruct the casualty's airway. If you suspect a mouth sting,

✚ CALL AN AMBULANCE

If possible, give the casualty ice cubes to suck or water to drink to minimise the swelling within the airway.

Snake bites

ADDER BITES

Common in many areas, the adder is the only poisonous snake native to Britain. To prevent poison from a bite spreading, keep the heart above the level of the wound.

SIGNS AND SYMPTOMS

- One or two small puncture marks.
- Pain, redness and possible swelling.

Aim

- To contain the poison.

You will need

- Soap and water
- Dressing
- Bandage
- Blanket/towels

1 Lay the casualty down

Lay the casualty down and reassure him.

2 Wash around the wound

If possible, wash around the wound with soap and water. Cover the area with a dressing and secure this with a conforming bandage.

3 Immobilise the injured area

Support and immobilise the injured area by padding around the affected limb with rolled-up towels or blankets.

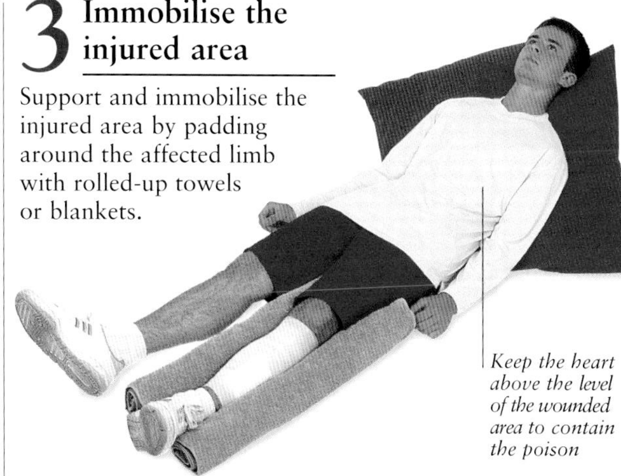

Keep the heart above the level of the wounded area to contain the poison

✚ CALL AN AMBULANCE

IMPORTANT
Keep the casualty calm and do not attempt to suck out the venom.

Marine injuries

JELLYFISH STINGS

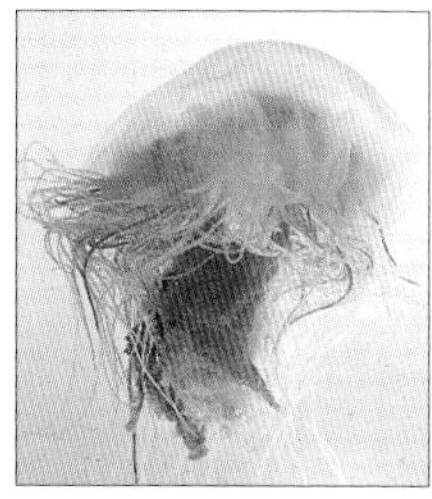

Many jellyfish found in temperate waters inflict painful stings. The poison is contained in stinging cells that stick to the skin and is released when each cell ruptures.

Treating a jellyfish sting

Pour vinegar over the area to inactivate the poison; dust with dry powder to stick the remaining cells together. Brush the powder off with a clean, non-fluffy pad.

WEEVER FISH STINGS

Weever fish have poisonous spines along their backs and are found around the British coast and elsewhere. The spines can puncture your foot, causing swelling and severe pain.

Treating a weever fish sting

Soak the foot in a bucket of water as hot as the casualty can bear until the pain eases. This will inactivate the poison.

EFFECTS OF TEMPERATURE

To enable our bodies to function properly, a body temperature of 36–37°C (97–99°F) must be maintained. In order to achieve this we adapt to different external conditions. When it is cold, we can retain heat by wearing warm clothes and create heat by eating high-energy foods. Our bodies lose heat in hot conditions through sweat evaporation (see p. 88), which can be helped by drinking plenty of fluid and wearing loose clothes. Exposure to extremes of temperature damages the skin and body tissues.

HYPOTHERMIA

This occurs when the body temperature drops below 35°C (95°F), for example, in very cold weather or on expeditions. It is often caused by wearing unsuitable clothes in cold weather or by prolonged immersion in cold water and can also result from being in a poorly heated or unheated room.

Elderly people and young babies are especially at risk; elderly people are less aware of changes in temperature and young babies do not have a fully developed temperature-regulating mechanism.

SIGNS AND SYMPTOMS

- ▶ Casualty may lose consciousness.
- ▶ Very cold and pale skin, shivering.
- ▶ Clumsiness, irritability, slurred speech.
- ▶ Slow breathing, weak pulse, lethargy.

FOR A CASUALTY INDOORS

Aim

- To stop loss of body heat.
- To rewarm the casualty.
- To obtain medical aid.

You will need

- Dry clothes
- Warm drinks and high-energy food

1 Replace wet clothing with dry, warm garments

If a casualty has been brought inside wearing wet clothes, replace these with dry clothes as soon as possible.

IF the casualty is young and fit, he or she can be rewarmed by taking a bath. The water should be a warm 40°C (104°F).

IF the casualty is elderly or is a young baby, rewarm the casualty by wrapping blankets around him or her.

2 Place the casualty in bed and give warm drinks

Get the casualty into bed and give him or her warm drinks, soup or high-energy foods such as chocolate. Cover the casualty's head for additional warmth.

☎ CALL A DOCTOR

FOR A CASUALTY OUTDOORS

Aim

- To stop the casualty's body temperature falling further.
- To make the casualty warmer.
- To get medical assistance.

You will need

- Survival bag, sleeping bag or blanket
- Warm clothes
- Warm drink

1 Rest the casualty immediately

Stop immediately and rest. Do not continue in the hope that you can find shelter for the casualty. Insulate the casualty with extra garments.

IF you have dry clothing available, replace all wet clothing with dry.

IF someone is with you, send him or her to get help.

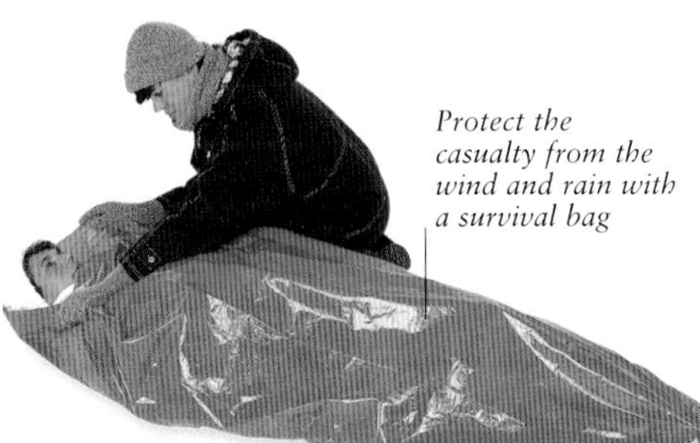

Protect the casualty from the wind and rain with a survival bag

2 Shelter and insulate the casualty

Make a shelter for the casualty to protect her from the elements. Wrap her in a survival bag, sleeping bag or a blanket. Lay her down on dry, insulating material such as dry heather or bracken.

▶ **DO NOT** use a hot water bottle or an electric blanket to attempt to warm the casualty.

▶ **DO NOT** give the casualty any alcohol to drink.

3 If possible, give the casualty a warm drink

Give the casualty a warm drink, such as milk, cocoa or soup, if available. Reassure and comfort her.

> **!** **IF** the casualty loses consciousness, check breathing and place him in the recovery position (see p. 18) or on his side. If necessary, be ready to resuscitate (see pp. 16–25).
>
> 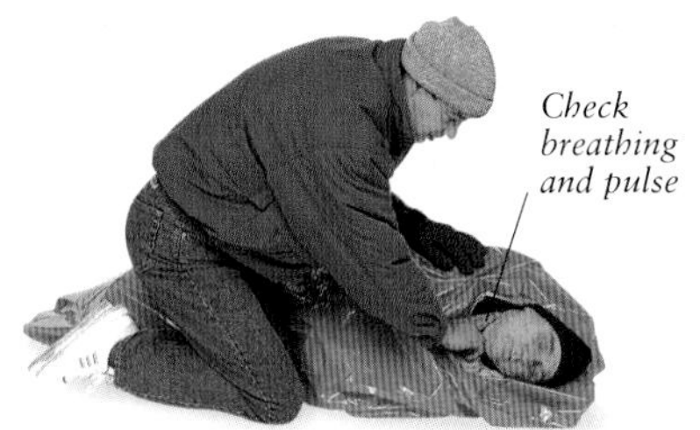
>
> *Check breathing and pulse*

4 Look for signs of frostbite

If the casualty appears to have frostbite (see p. 88) treat her accordingly.

5 Arrange for the casualty to be transported

Arrange to get the casualty to hospital – she must be carried on a stretcher. Do not let her walk or leave her alone.

FROSTBITE

This occurs when parts of the body, for example, the fingers or toes, become frozen due to intense cold. It may be accompanied by hypothermia (see p. 86).

SIGNS AND SYMPTOMS

- Prickling pain followed by gradual loss of feeling in the affected area.
- Affected skin will feel hard and turn white, then blue and finally black.

Aim

- To warm the affected area slowly in order to prevent further tissue damage.
- To obtain medical aid.

You will need

- Gauze bandage or dressing

► **DO NOT** thaw a frostbitten foot if further walking is necessary.

► **DO NOT** warm the frostbitten part with a hot water bottle.

1 Remove tight clothing

Remove any tight or constrictive clothing from around the affected part, for example, rings, gloves or boots.

2 Warm affected area slowly

The affected part should be warmed slowly. The casualty can put her hands in her armpits or put her feet in your armpits. Apply a loose dressing of a gauze bandage. Keep the affected area covered until colour and feeling return to the skin.

☐ TAKE OR SEND THE CASUALTY TO HOSPITAL

HEAT EXHAUSTION

This is a condition caused by an abnormal loss of salt and water from the body through excessive and prolonged sweating.

SIGNS AND SYMPTOMS

- Cramp-like pains and/or headache.
- Pale, moist skin.
- Fast, weak pulse.
- Slightly raised temperature.

Aim

- To cool down the casualty.
- To replace lost fluid and salt.

You will need

- Tumbler of slightly salty water

1 Lay the casualty down

Help the casualty to lie down in a cool place. Raise his legs to improve blood flow.

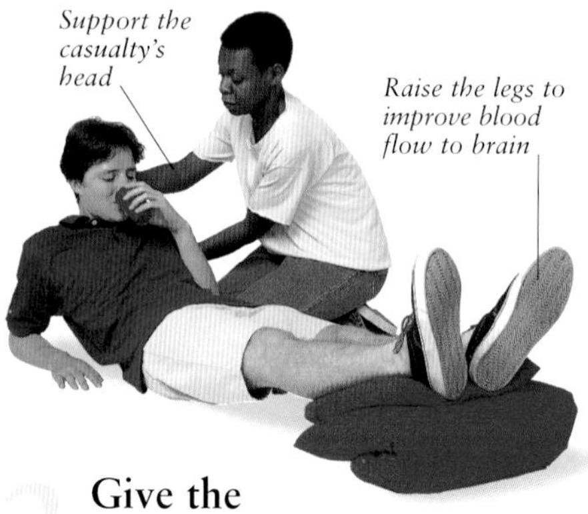

2 Give the casualty plenty of water

Give him plenty of water to drink; if possible, make the water slightly salted.

✚ CALL AN AMBULANCE

HEATSTROKE

This potentially dangerous condition occurs when the body is unable to cool itself by sweating, due to illness or prolonged exposure to heat and humidity. Common in tropical areas, it can also occur during hot spells in milder climates and particularly to people who exercise in hot weather.

SIGNS AND SYMPTOMS

- Restlessness.
- Casualty may have a headache and feel dizzy.
- Skin will be flushed and feel very hot.
- Rapid loss of consciousness.
- Fast, strong pulse.
- Body temperature will be raised and may reach 40°C (104°F) or higher.

Aim

- To lower the casualty's body temperature as quickly as possible.
- To get the casualty to hospital.

You will need

- Large sheet
- Water spray or watering can
- Fan, preferably electric (keep away from water)

1 If possible, wrap the casualty in a cold, wet sheet

Lay the casualty down in a cool place and remove his clothes. If available, wrap the casualty in a cold, wet sheet and keep it wet, or sponge his body down with cold or tepid water.

✚ CALL AN AMBULANCE

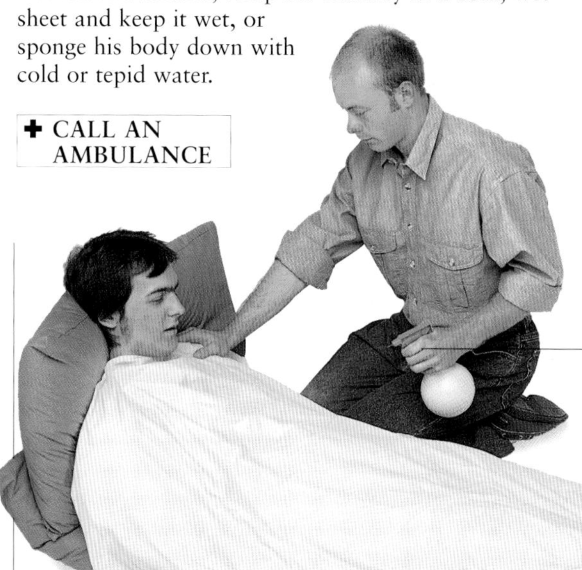

Continually sprinkle the sheet with water

Wrap the casualty in a wet sheet

2 Fan the casualty

Fan the casualty until his temperature falls to 38°C (100.4°F) under the tongue or 37.5°C (99.5°F) under the armpit.

3 Replace sheet with a dry one

When the casualty's temperature has fallen to a safe level, replace the wet sheet with a dry one.

4 Monitor the casualty

Regularly monitor the casualty until help arrives.

SMALL FOREIGN BODIES

A foreign body is any small object, such as a piece of gravel, a splinter or a shard of glass, that enters the body through a break in the skin or through one of the body's natural openings, such as the mouth, nose or ear. Children, in particular, sometimes swallow small peas or beads or push them into their ears or up their noses. Loose particles of dirt, in a graze for example, can usually be washed out or removed with gauze swabs (see p. 58) or with tweezers, as shown below.

SPLINTERS

The tiny pieces or slithers of wood, glass or metal that become embedded in the skin are the most common type of foreign body. Splinters are rarely clean and may cause infection. If a splinter is sticking out of the skin, remove it with tweezers as shown below. If the end of the splinter is not visible, a doctor or nurse should remove it because it is easy to push a splinter further in, making it harder to remove.

SIGNS AND SYMPTOMS

- The casualty may complain of pain where the splinter went into his hand.
- The cause of the injury may be nearby.
- The splinter is visible in the skin.

Aim

- To remove the splinter from the skin.
- To stop the wound becoming infected.

You will need

- Disposable gloves
- Tweezers
- Cold water
- Match or lighter

IMPORTANT

- **Never dig into the area to get at a small foreign body or splinter.**
- **Remember to keep your tetanus inoculations up-to-date.**

▶ **DO NOT** touch the wound with your fingers. Wear gloves, if possible.

1 Clean the wound

Rinse the area around the splinter with cold water. Before treating the casualty's wound, make sure that you wash your own hands thoroughly with soap and warm water (see p. 8).

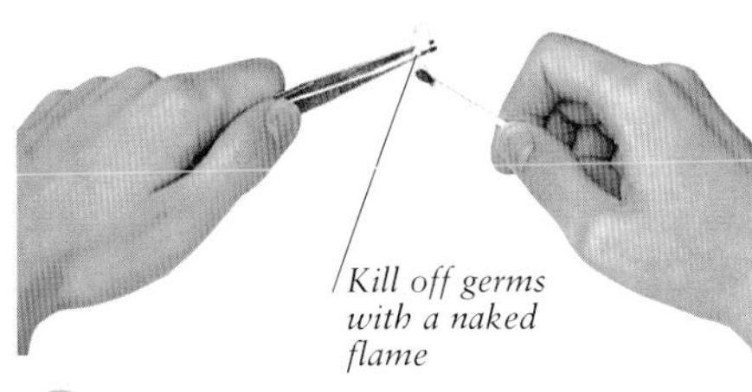

2 Sterilise the tweezers

Sterilise a pair of tweezers by passing them through the flame from a match or lighter. Allow the tweezers to cool.

► **DO NOT** wipe the soot off or touch the end of the tweezers.

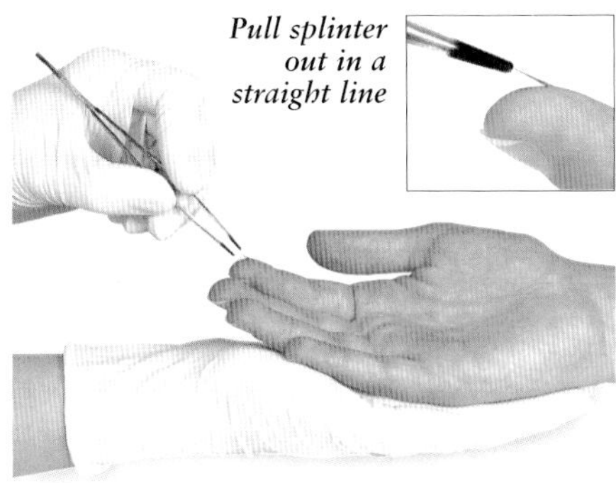

3 Pull the splinter out with the tweezers

Holding the tweezers as near to the skin as possible, grasp the end of the splinter. Pull the splinter out in a straight line at the same angle to which it entered.

IF the splinter breaks, do not carry on trying to remove it. An anti-tetanus inoculation may be necessary for the casualty to avoid an infection.

■ ADVISE THE CASUALTY TO SPEAK TO A DOCTOR

FISH HOOKS

Do not try to remove an embedded fish hook. Bandage around the hook and ensure that the casualty receives medical aid.

Aim

- To seek medical aid.

You will need

- Gauze pads
- Bandage

1 Cut the fishing line

Cut the fishing line. Try to cut the line as close as possible to the hook.

2 Build up pads of gauze

Put pads of gauze around the hook until you can bandage over it without pushing it in.

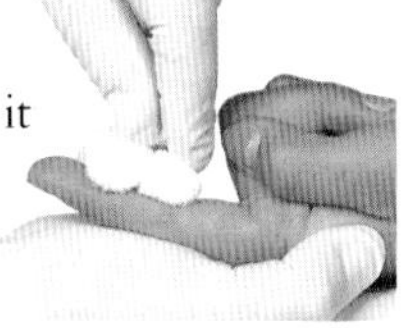

see *Embedded object* p. 52

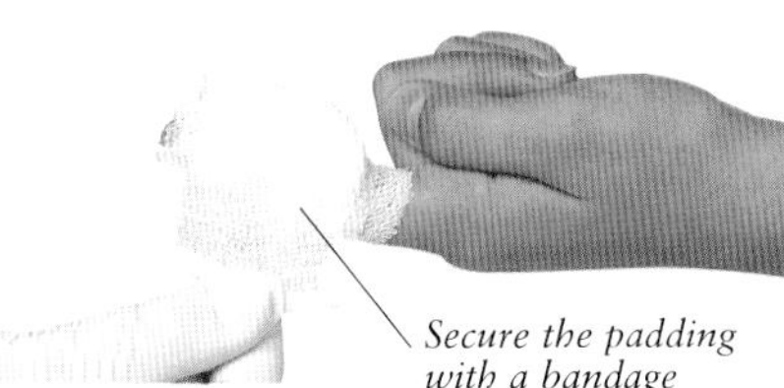

3 Bandage over the gauze padding

Bandage over the hook and the padding; take care not to press down on the hook.

□ TAKE OR SEND THE CASUALTY TO HOSPITAL

FOREIGN BODIES IN THE EYE

The most common foreign bodies found in eyes are pieces of grit or dust, eyelashes or small insects, and most are easily removed.

SIGNS AND SYMPTOMS

- Pain or discomfort, blurred vision.
- Redness, watering of the eye.

Aim

- To prevent injury to the eye.
- To remove the foreign object.

You will need

- Jug, bowl, water and towel
- Moist gauze pad or handkerchief
- Eyebath

▶ **DO NOT** remove anything from the coloured part of the eye or that is stuck in the eye. Cover the eye with a sterile dressing and get the casualty to hospital.

1 Sit the casualty down facing the light

Tell the casualty not to rub her eye. Ask her to sit down in a chair facing a light and to lean back slightly.

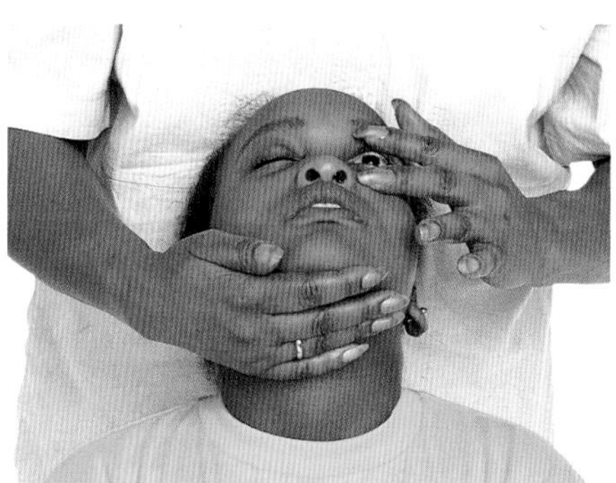

2 Examine the casualty's eye

Stand behind the casualty and ask her to look up. Supporting her chin, gently separate the eyelids and look for the object.

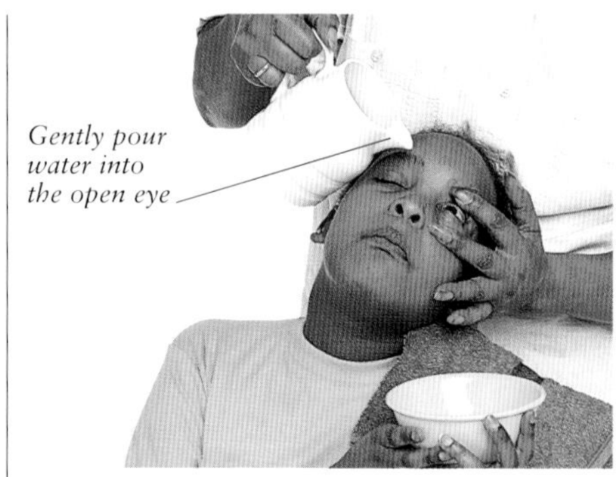

Gently pour water into the open eye

3 Remove the foreign body, if it is visible

If the object is visible inside the eyelid or on the white of the eye, pour water from a jug into the inner corner of the eye to flush it out. If this doesn't work, lift it off with a moist gauze swab or clean handkerchief.

4 Examine the upper eyelid

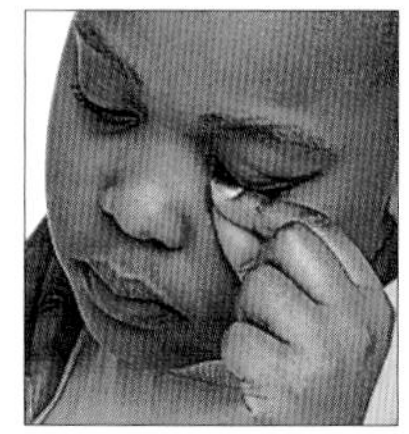

If the particle is under the upper lid, ask the casualty to look down, grasp her upper lid by the lashes and draw it out and down over the lower lid.

IF the object is still there, bathe the eye and ask her to blink; the object should float off.

! IF you have been unsucessful,

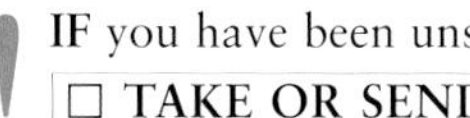

☐ TAKE OR SEND THE CASUALTY TO HOSPITAL

IN THE EAR

This is common in young children who have a habit of trying to put things into their ears. Sometimes, an insect may fly or crawl into a person's ear, which can cause distress. Foreign bodies in the ear can cause temporary deafness or may damage the eardrum.

Aim

- To prevent injury to the ear.
- To remove the foreign body.
- To obtain medical help if necessary.

You will need

- Towel
- Jug of tepid water

▶ **DO NOT** try to dig anything out of the ear, even if you can see it.

1 Reassure the casualty

Reassure the casualty. Advise her not to try to remove the object herself or to dig in the ear with her fingers.

2 Ask the casualty to tilt her head to one side

If an insect is in her ear, tell her to tilt her head to one side with the affected ear uppermost. Place a towel over her shoulder and support her head with your hand.

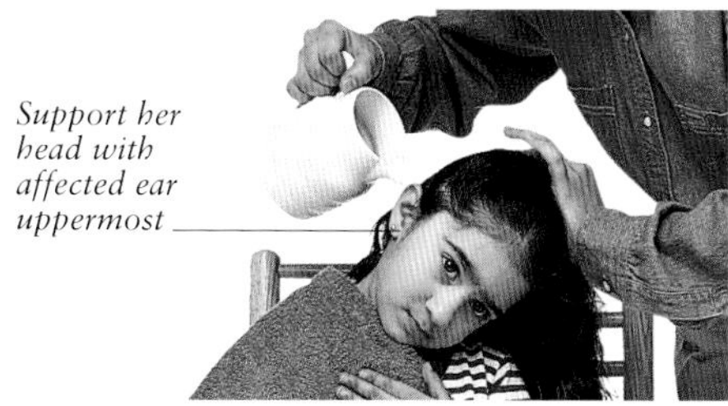

Support her head with affected ear uppermost

3 Float the insect out of the ear using tepid water

Gently pour tepid water into the ear. The insect should float to the surface.

IF a child has pushed something into her ear, tilt her head so that the affected ear is downwards; the object may drop out.

IF you cannot remove the object or insect from inside the ear,

☐ TAKE OR SEND THE CASUALTY TO HOSPITAL

IN THE NOSE

A common occurence with children, foreign bodies in the nose may cause blockage and infection.

SIGNS AND SYMPTOMS

- Difficulty breathing, or noisy breathing through the nose.
- Swelling of the nose.
- Smelly or bloodstained discharge coming from the nose.

Aim

- To reassure the casualty.
- To get medical attention.

Keep the casualty quiet and calm; tell him to breathe steadily through the mouth.

☐ TAKE OR SEND THE CASUALTY TO HOSPITAL

▶ **DO NOT** try to remove a foreign body with your fingers or an instrument, even if it is visible.

INDEX

A

B

C

D

E

F

G

H

I

J K

L

M

N

O

P

R

Acknowledgments

The authors would like to thank:

Dr Vivian Armstrong, Alesha Bailey, Sir Peter Beale KBE FRCP FFCM FFOM DTM&H, Lucia May, John Perry

Dorling Kindersley would like to thank the following:

Design assistance
Ian Merrill, Robert Newman

Editorial assistance
Fergus Collins

DTP assistance
Adam Moore, Rajen Shah

Illustrations
Halli Verrinder

Picture credits
Heather Angel, 85*bl*; Planet Earth Pictures, 85*br*

Models
Hayley Beatty, Dale Buckton, Ingrid Chen, Rae Chen, Declan Collins, Fergus Collins, Mark Cronin, Claire Cross, Edward Deeks, Estelle Dupart, Carole Evans, Anthony Ferretti, Eric Ferretti, Mary Ferretti, James Fraser, Siobhan Geoghegan, Les Goodrich, Joany Haig, Mei Hau, Amy Inman, Clara Inman, Peter Kelleher, Alison Kerl, Amanda Kernot, Alastair King, Natalie King, Olivia King, Andy Komorowski, Nina Loving, Brian Marsh, Maija Marsh, Nasim Mawji, Juliana Mendes-Ebden, Fario Mohammed, Hamida Mohammed, Jason Moran, Yemisi Ojutalayo, Mark Peters, Lucinda Rakes, Lorna Rhodes, Richard Shellabear, Peter Simmons, Mike Swinburne, Ellie Syllogides, Natalia Syllogides, Debbie Voller, Dominica Warburton

Makeup
Juliana Mendes-Ebden and also Jill Hornby and Alex Volpe

Additional photography
Gary Ombler, Steve Gorton

Index
Sue Bosanko

The British Red Cross Society, a registered charity, receives a royalty for every copy of this book sold by Dorling Kindersley. Details of the royalties payable to the British Red Cross can be obtained by writing to the Publisher, Dorling Kindersley Limited at 9 Henrietta Street, London WC2E 8PS. For the purposes of the Charities Act 1992, no further seller of the manual shall be deemed to be a commercial participator with the Society.

The British Red Cross cares for people in crisis at home and abroad. It gives vital impartial support during both major emegencies and personal crises, and provides comprehensive training in First Aid and caring skills. The red cross emblem is a symbol of protection during armed conflict and its use is restricted by law.